THE NILE BASIN

Richard F. Burton

THE NILE BASIN

and

Captain Speke's Discovery
of the Source of the Nile

by James Macqueen

New Introduction by

Robert O. Collins
University of California
Santa Barbara

DA CAPO PRESS • NEW YORK • 1967

A Da Capo Press Reprint Edition

This Da Capo Press edition
is an unabridged republication
of the first edition
published in London in 1864
by Tinsley Brothers

Library of Congress Catalog Card No. 65-23403

© 1967 Da Capo Press
A Division of Plenum Publishing Corporation
227 West 17 Street, New York, N. Y. 10011

Printed in the United States of America

INTRODUCTION

Sir Richard Burton defies definition. His seem-
ingly limitless abilities transcend any single
classification or simple explanation. He was an
exceptional linguist, having mastered at least
twenty-nine different languages by the end of
his life. He was a competent geographer, botanist,
geologist, meteorologist, archaeologist, and an-
thropologist. At one time or another he was a
soldier, inventor, author, and poet. His intellectual
accomplishments appear to have had no end. He
fastidiously observed and recorded everything
around him, and the chronicles based on his numerous travels are scholarly, thorough, and not infre-
quently dramatic and exciting. The voluminous
footnotes and appendices which burden his many
volumes testify to his passion for facts and statis-
tics, no matter how insignificant. Yet the narra-

tives of his travels rise above the clutter of pedanticisms and stand today with the best of adventure stories.

If Burton possessed many talents, however, he was above all a traveler. His passion for wandering was fed by a romantic fascination for the strange and exotic. He was an incurable romantic in an age of romanticism, but if that romanticism carried him to the ends of the earth, his judgments about the inhabitants of unknown lands were conditioned by Victorian ideas of progress and civilization. Thus, Burton could admire the Arabs while despising Africans. He was drawn to Arabia by his love of travel, yet it was the complexities of Arab culture that impressed him. The more he came to know the Arabs, the more he admired their civilization and respected their customs, manners, and hospitality, which he regarded as equal in sophistication to those of Victorian Britain. In 1853, while serving in the Indian Army, he disguised himself as a Pathan from Afghanistan and visited the Holy Cities of Mecca and Medina. His subsequent account of his exploits became an immediate bestseller.

Burton's insatiable appetite for travel soon brought him to Africa. He observed Africa and the Africans at best with the assumptions of a Victorian Englishman, at worst with the attitudes of an Arab slave trader. Not surprisingly, he judged African culture, which he made no attempt to understand, as hopelessly inferior to the Asian and European civilizations he knew so well. African customs, manners, and morals repulsed him, perhaps because they did not fit his preconceived notions of civilization. Moreover, he never sought to separate race and culture. Thus African cultural inferiority became obvious proof of African racial inferiority.

This "Afrophobia" led Burton, as well as other Englishmen, to place Africans at the bottom of the evolutionary scale of national and racial development.[1] True, Burton was sufficiently condescending to consider Africans human beings, but humans of the lowest kind. He argued that only through emigration, or, perhaps, by the adoption of Islam, could they hope for salvation. Burton's bigoted

---

1. C. W. Newbury, Introduction to Sir Richard Burton, *A Mission to Gelele, King of Dahome* (New York, 1966), p. 39.

ideas of African inferiority colored all of his writings about Africa, and the more he saw and learned, or rather mislearned, the more vicious became his contempt for the continent. One should not read Richard Burton without keeping in mind this deep-seated prejudice.

Although Burton disliked Africa and the Africans, his restless spirit and passion for travel in outlandish places brought him back more than once. He traveled to Somaliland first in 1854 and again in 1855. From 1857 to 1859, he made his famous journey to Lake Tanganyika with John Hanning Speke, and he served as the British Consul in West Africa from 1861 to 1864.

During his trip to Somaliland in 1854, Burton became the first white man to visit the forbidden city of Harar. He was accompanied to the coast by three fellow Indian Army officers, including Speke, who was later to play such an important role in his life.

In 1855, this same group returned to Somaliland, planning to journey from the coastal city of Berbera to the Nile by way of Harar. While encamped near Berbera on the night of April 18, the party was attacked by a Somali raiding party. The four Englishmen soon found themselves hopelessly outnumbered, and Speke began to move back toward the line of tents. Burton snapped at him to hold his ground, and Speke, interpreting the remark as a reflection on his courage, rushed forward at the enemy. One of the Englishmen was killed. Three survived, including Burton and Speke, both of whom were seriously wounded. All equipment and supplies were lost, and the journey had to be abandoned. The only lasting results of the abortive expedition were the scars of the wounded and Speke's damaged pride, which continued to fester long after his physical injuries had healed.

Following a short term of duty in the Crimean War, Burton returned to Africa in December, 1856. His intention was to seek the "Sea of Ujiji," which the Arabs had described and which Burton hoped would be the source of the Nile. He applied to the Royal Geographical Society of London for financial assistance, but upon the advice of the German explorer, Heinrich Barth, he did not mention the discovery of the Nile source in his proposal. He explained to the Society only that his purpose was to ascertain the existence of the inland lake called the "Sea of Ujiji," but there can be no doubt that he regarded this goal as a secondary aspect of the Nile quest. The Society approved the journey, even persuading the British Government to furnish one thousand pounds toward expenses; and the East India Company agreed to give Burton two years' leave of absence with full pay.

For a companion Burton again called upon John Hanning Speke, who at the time was in London planning a similar adventure. But whereas Burton was principally interested in travel, Speke was primarily concerned with hunting and collecting animals. He hoped to march to the Nile headwaters and then proceed downstream to the Mediterranean, shooting and capturing rare birds and animals along the way, the collection to be used ultimately to open a natural history museum in England.

Speke accepted Burton's invitation, and the two men arrived in Bombay in November, 1856, to gather the necessary supplies. Preparations went forward smoothly, and the expedition departed for Zanzibar in December. Although no outward signs of animosity were apparent between the two men, Speke had undoubtedly not forgotten the insult at Berbera, while Burton continued to belittle all those, including Speke, with lesser talents than himself.

The expedition reached Zanzibar on December 20, and matters immediately turned for the worse. Men and supplies were difficult to obtain, for the island was in a turmoil over the disputed accession of Sayyid Majid to the Sultanate. The British Consul, Atkins Hamerton, bedridden and near death, could give little assistance, and the explorers had to be content with preliminary excursions to the coast. In customary fashion, Burton spent much of the time learning the local language, Swahili.

Finally, after a delay of nearly six months, Burton and Speke embarked for Bagamoyo on the mainland on June 16, 1857. Here they spent ten days attempting to secure porters to carry the supplies. Few porters were available, and Burton, never much of a judge of men, took little care in their selection. In the end he managed to assemble a motley crew, consisting of servants, soldiers, and thirty-six porters. This was hardly an auspicious beginning to a difficult journey.

On June 26, the expedition marched out of Bagamoyo to the west. Burton followed the next day. The way west was a well-known slave route that led from Bagamoyo upcountry to Tabora (called Kazeh by Burton) some five hundred miles inland. Trouble began at once. On the first day three soldiers deserted. Burton proved incapable of establishing discipline among the men. They squabbled constantly, refused to carry out their assigned tasks, and often simply disappeared, usually with precious supplies. The fewer the men, the heavier the individual loads, but the stronger porters declined to carry more and left the extra weight to their weaker companions. Every few days the expedition was halted by local chieftains demanding tribute. A settlement often took hours to arrange, further delaying the caravan. Within a fortnight both Burton and Speke were stricken with malaria and periodically had to be carried in stretchers, adding to the loads of the already overburdened porters. Each day it became harder

to stop the quarrels among the men. Each morning
it took longer to organize the march. By July 14
the expedition had covered only 118 miles, less
than four and one half miles a day.

As the difficulties increased, so too did Burton's
contempt for East Africa and its people. He caus-
tically referred to the Africans as childish, im-
moral, lazy, and preoccupied with drunkenness.
He contemptuously described East Africa as a
land with ''few traditions, no annals, and no ruins,
the hoary remnants of past splendor so dear to
the traveller and the reader of travels. It contains not a single useful ornamental work of art,
a canal or a dam is, and has ever been, beyond
the narrow bounds of its civilization. It wants even
the scenes of barbaric pomp and savage grandeur
with which the student of Occidental Africa is
familiar.''[2] Never once did Burton stop to consider
that sophisticated cultures or the remains of advanced civilizations might be found beyond the
horizon to the north, or that the decay and degradation he witnessesd could be related to the Arab

2. Sir Richard F. Burton, *The Lake Regions of Central Africa*
(New York, 1961), *I*, pp. 106-107.

slave trade. Although the expedition frequently passed Arab slave caravans and saw the death and destruction left in their wake, Burton could never attribute the horrors to his beloved Arabs, arguing instead that the savagery of Africa was created by the nature of the Africans themselves. Speke suffered the same hardships and observed the same barbarism, yet he never drew the same conclusion. The fact that Burton possessed very acute powers of observation only makes his racism all the more curious.

On November 7, 1857, after five long months, the caravan finally reached Tabora, the principal inland center of the Arab slave trade. Burton was overjoyed to be among the Arabs once again. He acclaimed the striking "contrast between the open-handed hospitality and hearty good-will of this truly noble race, and the niggardness of the savage and selfish African—it was heart of flesh after heart of stone."[3] The Arabs helped him to find new porters, provided him with a house and food, and gave him valuable information. After a month the expedition had been refitted and made ready to

---

3. *Ibid.*, p. 323.

move west once again. For Burton, the weeks at Tabora among the Arabs were undoubtedly his happiest times in Africa.

On December 14, the expedition left Tabora on the final march westward to the "Sea of Ujiji." Once again the men quarreled and supplies and porters disappeared. Once again Burton and Speke were ill, Burton losing all feeling in his hands and feet, Speke suffering from an ophthalmia which virtually blinded him. Finally, on February 13, 1858, they reached the top of a hill, and Burton noticed something shining brightly below. They had reached the "Sea of Ujiji" at last, for beyond, glittering in the African sun, lay the brilliant waters of Lake Tanganyika.

As the expedition marched into the Arab trading post of Ujiji on the shores of the lake, Burton was already planning his next move. He had discovered a great lake in central Africa, and now he had to see if the lake was in fact the source of the Nile. If a river flowed northward from Lake Tanganyika, it would very likely be the Nile. Burton could then return in triumph to London, claiming to have solved the mystery of the Nile headwaters which had baffled mankind since antiquity.

After numerous difficulties, two large canoes were obtained, and on April 10, Burton and Speke set out for Uvira, the limit of Arab trading activities near the northern end of the lake. Once at Uvira, however, the Arab crewmen would go no further and spoke in fear of ferocious African tribes inhabiting the land to the north. Nor could the local Africans be induced to take the place of the Arabs, and twenty miles from his goal, Burton's Nile quest came to an end. He was bitterly disappointed and carefully questioned the inhabitants, who assured him that the river, the Ruzizi, flowed into the lake, and not out of it. This information turned disappointment to dismay, and Burton and Speke returned to Ujiji depressed and disconsolate. The Nile source remained unknown.

On May 28, the two travelers started back for Tabora, arriving on June 20. Here the expedition, halted to rest, recuperate, and refit. Burton took solace in again being among his Arab friends, chatting, gathering information, and compiling his notes. Since Speke knew no Arabic, he was left very much to himself, and when his health improved, he became restless. During their previous sojourn at Tabora, Burton and Speke had heard Arab reports of a lake directly north of Tabora larger even than Lake Tanganyika. Although the accounts of the two men conflict as to who actually proposed a journey to this lake, Speke left Tabora for the north on July 10 at the head of a small party.

Burton's decision not to accompany Speke proved to be the greatest mistake of his life. At one decisive moment, he lost the opportunity to become one of the great names of African exploration rather than simply an erudite but eccentric traveler. Burton had many reasons to remain at Tabora. He was exhausted and quite content to be rid of his companion, happy to reside with his Arab friends. Moreover, he thought that what had been accomplished already was sufficient, that his goals had been achieved. Ultimately, Burton was a traveler, concerned with completing his notes on what had been accomplished already, rather than an explorer, ever eager to press on to see what lay beyond the horizon; and this subtle but important distinction kept him at Tabora while Speke set out for the lake to the north which the Africans called Ukerewe.

On August 3, 1858, Speke reached Lake Ukerewe and recorded that "I no longer felt any doubt that the lake at my feet gave birth to that interesting river, the source of which has been the subject of so much speculation, and the object of so many explorers."[4] He named the lake "Victoria" in honor of his queen, remained three days on its southern shore, and then hastened back to Tabora. He arrived on August 25, and the next morning informed Burton of his discovery and his belief that he had found the source of the Nile. Burton reacted coolly to Speke's assertion. If it were true, Speke's discovery would overshadow all of his own investigations. But was it true? Speke had little evidence to support his claim. He had seen only a small part of the southern shore. He had not seen the spot where the Nile was supposed to debouch from the lake. He had estimated that it was a lake of great size because

---

4. "Captain J. H. Speke's Discovery of the Victoria Nyanza Lake, The Supposed Source of the Nile. From his Journal," Part II, *Blackwood's Edinburgh Magazine,* 86, October 1859, p. 412, col. 2.

it looked so and because a local African had told him so—hardly convincing evidence. Moreover, what Speke had seen did not take into account the "Mountains of the Moon" or the fact that Speke's lake might be only one in a series of lakes. To Burton and to others later on, there were simply too many alternate possibilities not accounted for in Speke's report. He felt, therefore, that the official report of the journey should emphasize Lake Tanganyika, of which they were certain, while omitting speculation on the sources of the Nile, of which they were not. Speke did not agree. After acrimonious wrangling, the two men decided not to discuss the subject until they reached England. But each was convinced that his own discovery was the significant result of the expedition, and each was prepared to present his case in London. Henceforth, relations between Burton and Speke steadily deteriorated, to end with inveterate hostility.

The expedition left Tabora late in September and reached Zanzibar in March, 1859. Within three weeks, the two men were on their way to Aden. The return journey had been anything but pleasant. Although outwardly friends, both Burton and Speke had been seriously ill and, in delirium, had lashed out at one another. By the time they reached Aden, each was glad to be rid of the other, and while Burton remained behind to rest, Speke left immediately for England. They parted as friends, however, Speke agreeing to say nothing about the expedition until Burton joined him in London. This was the last time that either was to acknowledge the friendship of the other.

Speke arrived in England on May 8. On the very next day, he went directly to the president of the Royal Geographical Society, Sir Roderick Murchison, and informed him of Lake Victoria and his belief that it was the source of the Nile. Murchison was impressed and invited Speke to address the Society. The press quickly learned of Speke's discovery, and a wave of Nilotic enthusiasm swept the British public. The Royal Geographical Society acted at once, deciding to send Speke back to Africa to determine that Lake Victoria was the Nile source. On May 21 Burton landed in England, only to learn that he had been outmaneuvered. The Society and the public displayed only polite interest in Lake Tanganyika and Burton's erudite and detailed scientific reports. He was not even invited to participate in the next expedition. All of his expectations had been crushed by Speke's breach of faith, and Burton sulked, a bitter man longing for revenge against his former companion.

Meanwhile, Speke was organizing a second expedition. He planned to strike out from Zanzibar, follow the same route as before to Lake Victoria, march up its western shore until he found the Nile outlet, and then trace the river northward to Egypt. As his partner he chose James Grant, a fellow Indian Army officer. Grant possessed the qualities of a perfect subordinate—modesty, an even temper, and complete devotion to his superiors. This time there would be no conflict of interests, and the Nile problem would be solved.

Speke and Grant arrived in Zanzibar in August, 1860, and after gathering the necessary supplies, set out for Lake Victoria. The caravan encountered the usual difficulties. Porters deserted, local chieftains demanded tribute, and Grant came down with malaria. As before, the expedition moved with incredible deliberation, and more than a year passed before Speke reached the Kingdom of Karagwe west of Lake Victoria.

Karagwe was one of a number of highly organized African states located west and north of Lake Victoria and known collectively as the Interlacustrine Bantu Kingdoms. These kingdoms possessed sophisticated cultures and state structures characterized by varying degrees of centralized government. Karagwe was ruled by King Rumanika, who greeted the first white men ever seen in his country on November 25, 1861.

Rumanika received his guests cordially, and they remained at his palace for more than a month. There Speke and Grant learned valuable information about the lake, which they had yet to see, and about the Kingdoms of Buganda and Bunyoro to the north. Buganda was ruled by an autocratic king, the Kabaka Mutesa, whose permission was required before the explorers could proceed. While waiting for Mutesa's consent, Speke passed the time inquiring into the customs and manner of living in Karagwe. Of particular amusement were Rumanika's obese wives. These women were force-fed on a constant diet of milk sucked from gourds through a straw until they were almost as wide as they were tall. They had become so fat that they could not stand and had to move by flopping about on all fours like walruses. When Speke attempted to measure one of them, he required the assistance of several men to get the woman to her feet. Once up, she quickly fainted from the strain.

In January, 1862, the explorers were allowed to advance into Buganda. Speke went on alone, while Grant, unable to walk, remained behind to recover, hoping to rejoin Speke within a short time. The journey to the Kabaka's palace took Speke six weeks. During it, he sighted Lake Victoria for the first time since he had stood on its southern shore in August of 1858.

Speke found the Kabaka Mutesa less friendly than Rumanika, and although he appears to have won Mutesa's respect, he was nevertheless kept a virtual prisoner in the palace until Grant's arrival three months later. Within the confines of the palace, Speke was well treated, being permitted to wander about freely recording his observations. Occasionally, the Kabaka would send him a young slave girl, and Speke would give her to one of his men for a wife. He gained the favor of the influential Queen Mother, who appears to have devoted much of her time to smoking, dancing, and drinking a banana beer called pombe.

During his stay, Speke learned from the Buganda that a little further to the east, a river emerged from Lake Victoria over a great waterfall. This was surely the Nile. As soon as Grant arrived, Speke determined to leave Mutesa's palace and press on to the river. Finally, after many frustrating delays, Mutesa agreed to let the explorers proceed. Quickly, the expedition made its way to the Nile, north of the lake. Here, curiously, the two explorers separated. Grant went north to open a way to the Kingdom of Bunyoro. Speke turned upstream to verify that it indeed issued from the lake. On July 28, he reached the falls, naming them Ripon Falls after the president of the Royal Geographical Society at the time his expedition had been approved. Speke was elated. "I saw that old father Nile without any doubt rises in the Victoria N'yanza, and, as I had foretold, the lake the the great source of the holy river which cradled the first expounder of our religious belief.''[5] He now had only to get home and tell the world of his discovery.

Speke marched north and overtook Grant. Together they entered Bunyoro, where they found the King, Kamrasi, suspicious and unfriendly. At Kamrasi's they learned of yet another large lake to the west called Luta Nzigi (known today as Lake Albert). From Bunyoro Speke and Grant continued northward, hoping to reach the Nile and then make their way downstream by water to Egypt. Travel was slow. Swamps and numerous rivers blocked the route, and by November the two explorers were weak and weary. A hope for relief remained, however. Before the expedition had left London, the Royal Geographical Society had granted one thousand pounds to John Petherick, the British Consul in the Sudan, to ascend the Nile and meet Speke and Grant with fresh supplies. Although they were already a year behind schedule, the explorers hoped that Petherick would be searching for them from his base at Gondokoro.

---

5. John Hanning Speke, *Journal of the Discovery of the Source of the Nile* (London, 1863), p. 467.

On February 15, 1863, the tired explorers reached Gondokoro. Instead of Petherick, they found the sportsman-adventurer, Samuel Baker, and his wife. Baker's was actually the last of three parties which had gone up the Nile to find Speke. An earlier expedition of three wealthy Dutchwomen had returned to Cairo, while Petherick and his wife had marched west of the Nile to purchase ivory after giving Speke up for dead. Tired and confused, Speke became enraged at Petherick. He mistakenly believed that the Consul had accepted the one thousand pounds from the Royal Geographical Society without intending to fulfill his obligations. When Petherick and his wife returned a few days later, Speke refused the supplies they had brought to Gondokoro for him at such great effort and informed them that he would journey to Khartoum on Baker's boat. The vindictiveness of an exhausted man fell on the hapless Petherick, and although Speke should have been satisfied by his recriminations at Gondokoro, his castigation of Petherick in his official report to the Royal Geographical Society was instrumental in Petherick's removal as British Consul. Nevertheless, despite this unpleasant, and unnecessary, incident, the two explorers were happy to have returned to a more familiar civilization. At the end of February they set sail for Khartoum and Cairo, proudly informing the Royal Geographical Society "that the Nile is settled!"[6]

In London, Speke and Grant received a tumultuous welcome. The Royal Geographical Society called a special meeting at which Speke was given a rousing ovation, and the crowd that gathered outside broke several windows in order to hear his talk. His book, *Journal of the Discovery of the Source of the Nile,* was an immediate success (contrary to Burton's claim that both editions were failures). But was the Nile settled? Many did not think so, and, not surprisingly, Richard Burton was foremost among them.

In 1860, Burton had published *The Lake Regions of Central Africa,* in which he charged that during their exploration of 1857–1859, Speke had disregarded the instructions from the Royal Geographical Society to inquire into the geography

---

6. Richard Burton and James Macqueen, *The Nile Basin, infra* p. 20.

of the "Sea of Ujiji" in order to make an illusionary discovery of the Nile source. Burton was not alone, and others soon began to question Speke's evidence. First, Speke claimed that he had found a large lake, yet he had seen the lake only at three different and widely separated locations— he had never circumnavigated it. Second, he proposed that the river which began at Ripon Falls was the same that joined the Blue Nile at Khartoum, yet he had not followed it throughout its course to verify this hypothesis. To many his evidence appeared entirely circumstantial, and the British public and scientific circles alike divided into those who favored Speke and those who did not. Clearly, the Nile Question was still on trial.

When Burton returned from West Africa in August, 1864, the controversy reached a climax, and the two explorers were invited to debate the Nile Question before the conference of the British Association for the Advancement of Science to be held at Bath in September. Both accepted.

The conference opened on September 15, and the two former companions saw one another for the first time since 1859. They refused to speak, confining their greetings to frigid stares. In the afternoon Speke appeared nervous and restless. In the middle of a session he exclaimed, "Oh! I can't stand this any longer," and left the room.[7] The following morning, the Members of Association filled the main hall to hear the debate. Burton was alone on the platform with his wife, Isabel. Speke did not arrive. After a considerable wait a member of the Association climbed to the platform to announce that Speke was dead. Upon his departure the previous day, Speke had gone hunting with his cousin and a gamekeeper. About four o'clock the cousin heard Speke fire his gun and turned to see him fall off a stone wall. He ran to find Speke dying with a large chest wound. In a few minutes the explorer was dead. The inquest ruled that Speke had been killed by an accidental discharge of his own gun.

Upon hearing the news, Burton was visibly shaken. According to his wife, he wept upon returning home. But if his grief were genuine, he quickly recovered to read a paper "On the

---

7. Quoted in Byron Farwell, *Burton* (New York, 1963), p. 241.

Present State of Dahome"; and although he had
not presented his speech on the Nile to the Association, Burton saw no reason why he should end
his attacks against Speke's claims regarding the
Nile source. On November 14, he spoke before the
Royal Geographical Society, giving the address
he had composed for the Bath meeting. Later in
the year he combined this lecture with James
Macqueen's reviews of Speke's *Journal* in the
Morning Advertiser and had them printed together under the title, *The Nile Basin*. This attack
on Speke and his claims was the culmination of
Burton's revenge against the man who five years
before had stolen his fame.

The Nile Basin is divided into two parts. The
first consists of a preface by Burton and his
speech to the Royal Geographical Society in November, 1864. The second is composed of Macqueen's reviews.

In his preface, Burton listed the principal criticisms of Speke's account. These were well known
at the time, and others had made them. During his
first journey to Lake Victoria, Speke, standing
some two hundred and fifty feet above the lake,

could see for about twenty miles, yet he claimed
upon returning that the breadth of the lake was
"eighty to one hundred miles" and that it was
the source of the Nile.[8] On his second journey,
Speke believed that he was marching around the
western perimeter of the lake, but he made no
attempt to verify this contention. Even while at
Rumanika's palace, he never traveled within sight
of the water only a short distance away. In all,
he followed the shore of his "vast" lake for no
more than fifty miles, thus allowing Burton to
argue that careful investigation would have shown
not one lake but two or more.

Similarly, after sighting Ripon Falls, Speke
immediately assumed that its waters descended
into the Nile, yet he followed the river north only
for fifty miles before leaving it to visit Kamrasi.
When he regained the river, he had missed nearly
ninety miles of its course, and after another fifty
miles, he again left it to strike out across country.
After bypassing at least one hundred and forty
miles of the course of his supposed Nile, he came

8. "Captain J. H. Speke's Discovery of the Victorian Nyanza
. . . ," *loc. cit.*, p. 414, col. 1.

upon a river which, once again, he simply assumed to be the one that began at Ripon Falls. Described by Speke as a "fine Highland stream," Burton concluded that it could hardly be "the *great* Nile stream" which flowed out of Lake Victoria at the falls.[9]

These were legitimate criticisms. In 1864 they clearly demonstrated that the Nile Question was not yet settled. Yet they were all negative accusations. They ignored Speke's great contributions to African exploration, belittling his work by citing evidence even more questionable than his own, and employing hearsay, facile insinuation, and personal innuendo. In the end, Burton was reduced to proclaiming the importance of his own East African journey, to asserting that the "line had been opened by me to Englishmen, and they had but to tread in my steps,"[10] and, finally, to lamenting that, except for a few esteemed friends, this vital service had been ignored or forgotten by all. This pitiful plea betrays the vengeance which

---

9. Speke, *Journal of the Discovery of the Source of the Nile,* pp. 468, 598.

10. *The Nile Basin, infra,* p. 27.

drove Burton to prove Speke in error, for so long as people accepted Speke, Burton's work would remain of minor importance. It was hardly a creditable performance for Sir Richard Burton.

Burton did not, however, rely solely on negative criticism in his attempt to destroy Speke's claims. If Speke were to be proven wrong conclusively, a more satisfactory explanation, a positive one, would have to be set forth. This was the tactic Burton had intended to employ at the Bath meeting. Rather than assault Speke directly with the well-known arguments against his claims, he would present a cogent, well-reasoned theory of the Nile source that would relegate Speke's proposition to the limbo of myth. Unable to do so at Bath, Burton introduced his theory to the Royal Geographical Society at their November session and to the public in *The Nile Basin.*

In the past Burton had argued that there were many possible Nile sources that had yet to be eliminated. In *The Nile Basin,* however, he proposed that Lake Tanganyika was the western source and a lake named Bahari Ngo the eastern source. Although the Africans at Uvira had emphatically told Burton that the Ruzizi River flowed into Lake Tanganyika, he now decided in London that they were wrong. Besides, he asserted, many of the Arabs at Ujiji had reported the opposite, and everyone knew that they were the more trustworthy. Instead of asserting that Lake Tanganyika was the direct source of the Nile, however, Burton developed a connection between Lake Tanganyika and Lake Luta Nzigi, situated west of Bunyoro. Thus, Lake Tanganyika became the western "lake-feeder" of the Nile, since Burton had claimed, curiously, that a lake cannot be a source of a river. The eastern "lake-feeder" was Lake Bahari Ngo, which received its waters from the "Mountains of the Moon." Speke's Lake Victoria, in fact at least two lakes, was irrelevant to the Nile source. Only the virtuosity of Burton's imagination could have created so much geographical myth on so little evidence.

If Burton's criticisms were as just as his own hypothesis was spurious, James Macqueen's reviews of Speke's *Journal of the Discovery of the Source of the Nile,* reprinted from the *Morning Advertiser,* were as malicious as they were unedifying. James Macqueen (1778-1870) began his interest in geography as manager of a sugar plantation in the West Indies, where he collected information from African slaves about their homelands. In 1821 he returned to Britain, where, as editor of the *Glasgow Courier,* he defended the interests of the West Indian planters. He eventually settled in London and by his writings and correspondence with the Royal Geographical Society, acquired a reputation as an expert on African geography, although he had never seen the continent. Although Burton thought the reviews displayed an "inimitable dryness of style," they were actually slanderous, personal attacks against Speke devoid of any relevant facts or logical arguments.[11] They were designed to invalidate Speke's claims by ridiculing his account and assassinating his character. Macqueen heaped disgust on Speke's measurement of one of Rumanika's wives and derided his discovery of the lost land of Buganda, where "licentiousness and profligacy prevail to an unlimited extent."[12] He accused Speke of being

---

11. *The Nile Basin, infra,* p. 30.
12. *The Nile Basin, infra,* p. 68.

so busy accepting gifts of naked girls from the Dowager Queen that he had no time to journey to the lake to see if it were there. He attempted to trap Speke by emphasizing that his figures seemed to make the Nile run uphill. He branded him a "Philadelphia lawyer" and concluded by enumerating Speke's accomplishments: "The sacrifice and ruin of zealous associates—a mass of intelligence, if such it can be called, so muddled and confused in everything that we really believe he himself cannot find his way in it. Nor is this all; he came back with tales of great empires and polished states in Africa . . . ," which have turned out to be "mere moonshine. Those great empires have dwindled to atoms; barbarous, rude, savage, and ignorant beyond all precedent and example." Speke brought back nothing of any value or consequence. "It might, it ought to have been different. But the only person to blame for the poor results is Captain Speke himself."[13]

As a contribution to the resolution of the Nile Question, Macqueen's reviews were of little value.

---

13. *The Nile Basin, infra,* pp. 193-194

Today, they serve principally as evidence of the acrimonious and personal character of the debate over this question in mid-Victorian Britain.

Santa Barbara, California   Robert O. Collins
August 1966

THE NILE BASIN.

PART I.

SHOWING

TANGANYIKA TO BE PTOLEMY'S WESTERN LAKE RESERVOIR.

A MEMOIR READ BEFORE THE ROYAL GEOGRAPHICAL SOCIETY,
NOVEMBER 14, 1864.

WITH PREFATORY REMARKS.

BY RICHARD F. BURTON, F.R.G.S.

———◆———

PART II.

CAPTAIN SPEKE'S DISCOVERY OF THE SOURCE OF THE NILE.

A Review.

BY JAMES M'QUEEN, ESQ., F.R.G.S.,

AUTHOR OF A " GEOGRAPHICAL SURVEY OF AFRICA."

(REPRINTED BY PERMISSION FROM THE "MORNING ADVERTISER.")

LONDON:

TINSLEY BROTHERS, 18, CATHERINE ST., STRAND.

1864.

TO

THOSE KIND FRIENDS,

ESPECIALLY TO THOSE MEMBERS OF

THE ROYAL GEOGRAPHICAL SOCIETY

WHO HAVE AIDED AND ENCOURAGED ME TO COME FORWARD WITH

This Statement,

THE FOLLOWING PAGES ARE

AFFECTIONATELY INSCRIBED.

RICHARD F. BURTON.

ADVERTISEMENT.

THE reader is respectfully requested to observe that I have Five main Objections to the present " settlement " of the Nile question by deriving the great river from the supposed " Victoria Nyanza Lake :"—

There is a difference of levels in the upper and in the lower part of the so-called Lake. This point is important only when taken in connection with the following.

The native report that the Mwerango River rises from the hills in the centre of the so-called Lake.

The general native belief that there is a road through the so-called Lake.

The fact that the southern part of the so-called Lake floods the country for thirteen miles, whereas the low and marshy northern shore is not inundated.

The phenomenon that the so-called Lake swells during the dry period of the Nile, and *vice versâ.*

RICHARD F. BURTON.

CHURCHILL HOUSE, DAVENTRY,
Nov. 21, 1864.

καὶ μὴν καὶ παρὰ τῶν ἀπὸ τῆς ’Αραβίας τῆς Εὐδαίμονος διαπεραιουμένων ἐμπόρων ἐπὶ τὰ ’Ραπτὰ . . . μανθάνομεν . . . τὰς λίμνας δὲ ἀφ’ ὧν ὁ Νεῖλος ῥεῖ . . . ἐνδοτέρῳ σύχνῳ.—*Ptol.*, lib. i. ch. i. 17.

We learned from traders who passed over from Araby the Happy to Rhapta
. . . the lakes out of which the Nile flows . . . deep in the interior.

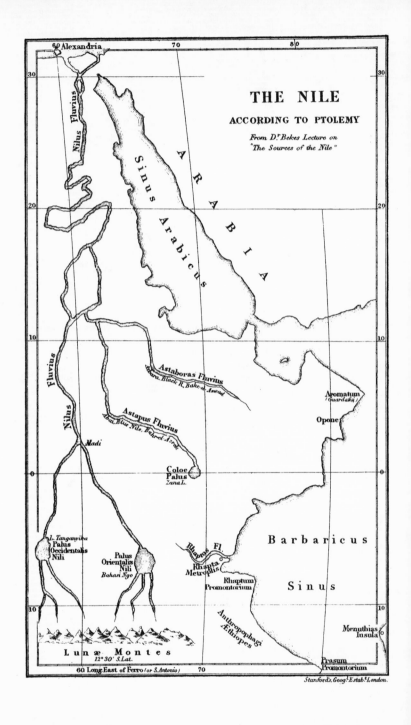

THE NILE

ACCORDING TO PTOLEMY

From D.ʳ Bekes Lecture on
"The Sources of the Nile"

A R A B I A

Sinus Arabicus

Nilus Fluvius

60 Alexandria

Fluvius

Nilus

Astaboras Fluvius
Atbara, Black R, Bahr-el-Aswad

Astapus Fluvius
Abai, Blue Nile, Bahr-el-Azrak

Madi

Coloe
Palus
Zana I.

Aromatum
(Guardafui)

Opone

L. Tanganyika
Palus
Occidentalis
Nili

Palus
Orientalis
Nili
Bahari Ngo

Rhapus Fl

Rhapta
Metropolis

Rhaptum
Promontorium

B a r b a r i c u s

S i n u s

Anthropophagi
Æthiopes

Menuthias
Insula

Lunæ Montes
12° 30' S.Lat.

Prasum
Promontorium

60 Long. East of Ferro *(or S.Antonio)* 70

Stanford's Geog.ˡ Estab.ᵗ London.

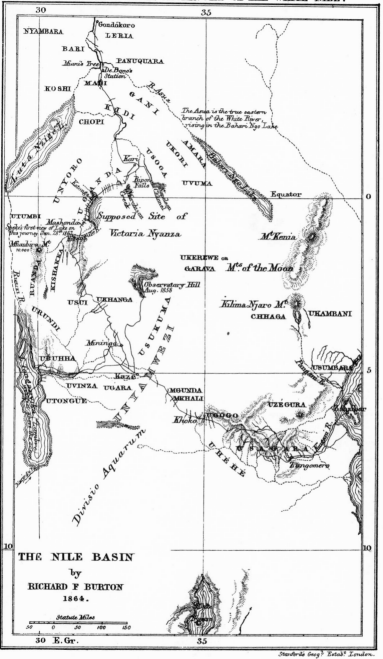

THE NILE BASIN
by
RICHARD F BURTON
1864.

PREFATORY REMARKS.

I HERE propose to write a few lines of introductory matter to a Memoir which was read by me before the Royal Geographical Society, on November 14th, 1864, and which is now published with more of detail. It is, however, still a notice purely geographical of a paper, "The Upper Basin of the Nile, from Inspection and Information," by my late lamented companion, Captain J. H. Speke, F.R.G.S., published in the Journal of the Royal Geographical Society, vol. xxxiii., 1863.

The melancholy event of September 15th, 1864, which cast a gloom over our meetings at the pleasant "Bath Association," precludes the possibility of my entering into any questions of a private or a personal nature. It would, of course, have been far more congenial to my feelings to have met Captain Speke upon the platform, and to have argued out the affair before the scientific body then assembled. I went down fairly to seek this contest on September 13th.

The day for the discussion was appointed for September 16th. Some hundreds of persons were assembled in the rooms of Section E, and when I appeared there it was only to hear that my quondam friend and Nile rival had on the previous afternoon lost his life by the merest accident. I had seen him at 13.0 P.M.; at 4 P.M. he was a corpse During the first shock caused by this most painful announcement I could not command myself to speak on the subject. Being now about to leave Europe for some years, during which the Nile question will have greatly changed its present aspect, I cannot, in justice to the public, as well as to myself, allow errors—of late almost generally received—to make further way. This is the object of the present volume. At the same time, be it distinctly understood that, whilst differing from Captain Speke upon almost every geographical subject supposed to be "settled" by his exploration of 1860-63, I do not stand forth as an enemy of the departed; that no man can better appreciate the noble qualities of energy, courage, and perseverance which he so eminently possessed than I do, who knew him for so many years, and who travelled with him as a brother, until the unfortunate rivalry respecting

the Nile Sources arose like the ghost of discord
between us, and was fanned to a flame by the enmity
and the ambition of " friends."

      ✻   ✻   ✻   ✻   ✻

I wish in no way to depreciate the solid services
rendered to geography by the gallant and adventurous
travellers, Captains Speke and Grant. They brought
us in an absolute gain of some 350 geographical
miles—between S. lat. 3° and N. lat. 3°,—before
known by only the vaguest reports. When, however, the bulletin of the French Geographical Society
(p. 266, tome vi. of 1863) speaks out so boldly upon
the moot question of the Nile Sources, it hardly
becomes English geographers to hold back. It is
now, I believe, the opinion of scientific Europe that
the problem is wholly unsolved, and, more still, that
within the last four years the Nile Basin has acquired an amount of fable which it never had in the
days of Pliny and Ptolemy.

A brief notice of the circumstances under which
the second expedition of our Society was formed is a
preliminary indispensable towards defining its results.
The day after his return to England (May 9th, 1859)
Captain Speke was induced to call at the rooms of

the Royal Geographical Society, and to set on foot a
new exploration. Having understood that he was
to await my arrival in London before appearing in
public, I was too late with my own project. This was
to enter Eastern Africa *viâ* the Somali country, or
by landing at the Arab town of Mombas, whence the
south-eastern watershed of the Nilotic Basin might
be easily determined. My offer was not preferred by
the Council of the Royal Geographical Society. I
have, however, every reason to believe, even by the
testimony of the last expedition, that the Mombas
line was in every way superior. With this opinion
the learned M. V. A. Malte Brun coincides.

Captain Speke left England on April 27th, 1860,
and set out definitively from Zanzibar on September
25th of the same year. On January 23rd, 1861,
the traveller arrived at our old dépôt, Kazeh, in
Unyamwezi, about S. lat. 5°. In 1858 he had
marched from that point northwards, and after 300
direct, or 425 indirect, miles, covered in forty-seven
days, from July 9th to August 25th, he sighted a
water of whose existence he had heard from Arabs
as well as Africans. Standing 250 feet above the
lake, which some called Ukerewe, and the others by

the generic name, Nyanza—sea, ford, or stream, in
fact, like Nyassa, the southern lake, it means simply
a water—he saw 20 to 22 miles of water breadth ; not
enough, indeed, to command a liquid horizon between
the islands, which he calls Mazita, Ukerewe, and Majid, and certainly not, as he states, " over 100 miles"
(*What led to the Discovery of the Sources of the
Nile*, p. 311). He returned to me at Kazeh, convinced that he had lifted the veil of Isis, that he had
discovered in that " broad open lake," not only the
" sources of some great river,' but the SOURCES OF
THE NILE. Now, rivers do not arise in lakes,
especially when lakes have extensive inundations; and
Captain Speke distinctly reported, after his first expedition to that water, that the Nyanza, being nearly
flush with the surface of the level country to the
south, shows signs of overflowing for some 13
miles during the rains.* I soon found the subject

* During the second expedition he found no signs of overflowing on the marshy lands to the N. and N.W. of the lake. This
circumstance, combined with 400 feet of difference in the level of
the surface of his Victoria Nyanza, speaks for itself. At our
opening *séance* of the Royal Geographical Society for 1864, Dr.
Murie asserted that such inundation might take place by supposing
a gorge at the north of the Luta. We should like to hear more
upon that subject from the learned gentleman.

too sore for discussion. Captain Speke never re-
flected that the more my expedition did, the better
for me. Presently I detected, by means of Arab
travellers, many minor errors in his actual exploration, such as making Mazita, and perhaps Ukerewe,
islands instead of a peninsula. Nor could I hear
anything, beyond the old legend which almost all
African tribes possess, touching ships' logs, sextants,
or white men near the head of the Nile, of which
none of my informants had heard. The Arabs of
Kazeh equally ignored the familiar tribal names of
Nyam Nyam, Bahri (Bari), Kidi, Shilluks, and
Dinkas. Also, in his original sketch, Captain Speke
carried his Victoria Nyanza to N. lat. 2° (*Lake
Regions of Central Africa*, p. 206, &c.). Finally,
the season of the Nile inundation (as I have stated in
the *Lake Regions of Central Africa*, vol. ii., p. 218)
peremptorily forbade the belief that the Nyanza is an
important feeder of the White Nile. That river in
Egypt floods in June and falls in December;
allowing time for the water to flow, it is therefore full
during the dry season, and low during the rainy season
south of the equator. About the Tanganyika Lake,
rain falls only during the six months when the sun is

in its southern declination.   For in Unyamwezi, as in
Congo, the rains divide the year into two unequal
portions of eight and four months, namely, the wet
season, which commences with violence in September and ends in May ; and the dry hot season,
which rounds off the year.

In the sketch-map prefixed to these pages, I have
shown all that is actually known of the so-called
" Victoria Nyanza."   The result is a blank space
covering nearly 29,000 miles, and containing possibly half a dozen waters. Its disappearance is
startling, but it has not been made to disappear
without ample reason.   We can accept only the
southern part seen by Captain Speke when he was
despatched from Kazeh, whilst I prepared for a
toilsome march upon Kilwa, and the north-western
water which he touched in January—July, 1862.
He brought home, as his original sketch-maps show, a
long parallelogram extending from north to south,
and ending in the latter direction with a kind of
triangle, whose arms fell in from the north-east and
north-west.   This triangle was the only portion that
he actually sighted ; and a simple protraction of its
arms, with a horizontal shore-line connecting their

extremities, is the secret of the present Victoria Nyanza's recognised and official shape.

On his second expedition, Captain Speke left Kazeh in the middle of May, 1861, and travelled to the north-west, holding so strongly by his preconceived ideas of the line of march lying parallel to *the* lake that he never was at pains to ascertain it was there. He might have visited it when living with King Rumanika of Karagwa, but he did not. After that time he turned to the north bending east, and on January 28, 1862, he sighted a water, which he at once instinctively determined to be *the* Nyanza. In vain the chiefs and people assured him that there were two lakes, and not one; and even asked him why he had not marched across his own lake instead of walking round it? And as he records in his Journal these remarks which could not disperse fore-gone conclusions, his evidence has been justly called " insufficient and inconclusive."

Captain Speke, shortly after leaving Rumanika, crossed the Kitangule River, a large stream running from S.W. to N.E. It is difficult to understand by his Journal at how many places he actually touched the supposed Nyanza, although it appears from his map that he perceived it at Mashonde and at Mashaka, and that he continued in sight of it as far as the Katonga River, a total of 50 geographical miles. The only actual record is at page 390 of his Journal, where, at Murchison Creek, he walks over hills and swamps to the west side of the lake, and is conveyed across the mouth of a deep "rush-drain" to the royal yacht establishment of Uganda. The red route-line on Captain Speke's Journal-map, running from Murchison Creek to the Ripon Falls, is a mere mistake; neither of the travellers saw a mile of the ground.

Thus the *Westminster Review*, No. 50, April, 1864, p. 315, distinctly asserts, that "on his first journey, in 1858, Captain Speke merely visited the southern extremity of the lake in about 2° 30′ S. lat. On his second journey, he and Captain Grant, though they skirted the north-western side of the lake, did not reach it except at the Murchison Creek, in 0° 21′ 19″ N. lat., and 32° 44′ 30″ E. long. . . . . so that, in point of fact, the Nyanza was actually visited at only two points, the one at the north, the at the south end." Besides, had Captains Speke and Grant really seen — which they did not — the three sides of *the* Nyanza, they would have left wholly unexplored 50,000 square geographical miles, a space somewhat larger than England and Wales. A careful survey was necessary before joining with the Nyanza the Bahari-Ngo or Baringo Lake. Captain Speke, whilst assuring his readers that the Asua—on a former occasion he had called it the Usua—River, which drains the latter into the Tubiri, Meri, or Upper White Nile, cannot be connected with the former, actually runs the two reservoirs into one. Thus, without counting the Katonga Valley,* he gives a fourth great outlet to his Victoria Nyanza, the others being two large water-courses which he calls " rush-drains," and makes to feed the main stream, or White Nile. These three effluents were found at the north-western corner of *the* lake, within a little more than 60 miles, a phenomenon which will not readily be

---

* The *Journal*, pp. 277—278, makes this feature wholly unin-telligible; the water in the " succession of rush-drains is always lowest when most rain fell" (?). " There is no doubt that they flowed into the lake [*i.e.*, to the S. E.], as I could see by the trickling waters in some few places [is that a test ?] ;" yet just outside the valley the " rush-drains were going to northward "— the opposite way.

accepted by geographers. It is far easier to believe in three independent lakes or widenings of rivers, which, the traveller owns, never exposed to him " a broad surface."

On July 19th, 1862, Captain Grant, without valid apparent reason, was sent to the head-quarters of King Kamrasi, of Unyoro, lying in 1° 37' N. lat. to the N.W., and away from the lakes. Captain Speke, apparently determined alone to do the work,[*] marched from Urondogani southwards to the place where the river, which he believed to be the White Nile, issued from the supposed Nyanza Lake. There again no sea horizon was seen. After following the stream about 50 miles to the northward from the Ripon Falls, he left it and rejoined Captain Grant. Both travellers proceeded together to Chaguzi, the palace of King Kamrasi, at the confluence of two effluents from the supposed Nyanza, the Kafu,[†] and

The *Westminster Review* (*loc. cit.*, p. 346) remarks of this feat: "But Grant will have little to regret, and Burton will be more than avenged, should Tanganyika and not Nyanza prove to be the head of the Nile."

† The Kafu is a continuation of the Mwerango River, which Captain Speke was informed rose amongst hills to the south. Thus the hills were in his own lake, " Victoria Nyanza."

the supposed White Nile, of whose bed 80 to 90 miles, between Urondogani and Chaguzi, were left unvisited.

From Chaguzi, Captains Speke and Grant again followed the stream for 50 miles as far as the Karuma Falls, in 2° 15′ N. lat. The " Nile." bending to the N.W., they left it at a considerable distance, and marched northwards 1° 25′ = 85 miles. Thus nearly 140 miles of stream issuing from the supposed Victoria Nyanza were left entirely doubtful. After much delay and many mistakes, they presently came upon the lower course of what was supposed to be the stream which they had left higher up. But, in truth, they had lost all traces of it. The people consulted by Captain Speke " would or could not tell him where the stream had gone to." He believed the Nile to be not far off (p. 585), yet, do or say what he would, everybody declared it was fifteen marches distant, and that it could not be visited under a month. Captain Speke, however, " knew in his mind all the reports were false," and the very first march from Faloro " brought him to Paira, a collection of villages within sight of the Nile." It is evident from his map that the supposed

White River, which may have been his own Kivira,* or other stream, discharged itself into the "Little Luta Nzige"Lake, afterwards decreed to be a "backwater." Instead however of *beating* the stream, Captain Speke had clearly missed it: it might easily have been drained by the Jur (Djour), which runs parallel to the White River, or by a similar branch into the Bahr el Ghazal, lately visited by Mr. Consul Petherick. Captain Speke's explanation of this peculiar phenomenon, and the exceeding difficulties into which that explanation has led him, will be found in the following pages.

The task of settling the many points touching the

---

* Given, like the Katonga and the Kitangule, as an influent to the Lake Nyanza in Captain Speke's map protracted in the field, and now in the hands of Mr. Findlay, F.R.G.S. It is suspiciously like the name Kira, the region west of the so-called Napoleon Channel. Mr. Findlay, I believe, first suggested that it would be better to make the Kivira an effluent flowing to Gondokoro. Captain Speke (*What led to the Discovery*, &c., p. 258) says : "The (Usoga) man (at Kazeh) called the river Kivira, and described it as being much broader, deeper, and stronger in its current than either the Katonga or the Kitangule River ; that it came from the lake, and that it intersected stony hilly ground on its passage to the N.W." All this is simply an after-thought, as a reference to Captain Speke's original map will show. Yet in his *What led to the Discovery*, &c., p. 308, he boasts that this map, prepared before leaving Unyanyembe, was "so substantially correct that in its general outlines he had nothing whatever to alter." Let the reader compare them.

"Luta Nzige" mystery has been left to Mr. Baker, who, by letter dated "Khartoum, June 8th, 1864," was reported to have arrived at Kamrasi's palace.

A little beyond Apuddo, in lat. 3° 34′ 33″, near the confluence of the Asua and the White Nile, Captain Speke (Journal, &c., p. 592) " at once went to see the tree said to have been cut by an Englishman some time before," and he found " something like the letters M. I." In the map it seems placed *to the west* of "the Nile." M. Miani, an Italian traveller, who has lately organised a fresh expedition for exploring the Asua River, marked his extreme point 1° 34′ 33″, or 94·5 miles further south. He says distinctly (*Commercio d'Egitto* of Cairo, Sept. 22nd and 24th), " My name, as marked upon Captain Speke's chart, does not occur at the position assigned to it, but much farther to the south, in fact at the 2nd degree of N. latitude *on the eastern bank* of the river, in the country of the Galuffi, whereas they (Captains Speke and Grant) place it on the left or western bank without naming any adjacent city." M. Miani further declares that some envious person pointed out to the explorers the tree where it is not. I have lately seen his sketch-map, sent to the Royal Geographical Society, in which he calls the " Lower Asué" the "Meri River."

If this be true, what becomes of the confluence of the Asua and the so-called White Nile ? Every attention should have been paid to the former, which is dismissed in a few words, merely telling us that the expeditionists sent up the Nile by Mohammed Ali had given an exaggerated account of its volume, and had fallen 20 miles short of their own "farthest point." But travellers ascending a stream are generally better judges of the main line than those descending, and of late years all explorers upward bound have pointed to the Asua or upper waters of the Tubiri or Meri as the True Nile. Mr. Petherick, I am informed, makes, after measurement, the volume of Asua nearly equal to that of the main line of the Nile. In p. 598 of his Journal, Captain Speke compares what he believes to be the true Nile with " a fine Highland stream," in fact a kind of " creek," which seems a queer main drain for his mighty Nyanza. Besides, Captain Speke makes in his own map the Asua to be the great south-eastern fork of the White Nile, and the main drain of the Bahari-Ngo Lake. Whether this feature does or does

not exist in the size now attributed to it, the Asua
proceeds directly from the north-western water-shed
of the giant peaks which represent, I believe,
Ptolemy's Lunar Range. It is there fed by the Œthi-
opic Olympus, Kitima-Njaro, whose height (20,000
feet) and whose snows are at length attested by Baron
Carl von der Decken. That enterprising traveller
has again proposed to enter East Africa by one of
the many streams—the Jub, the Ozi, or the Sabaki—
falling into the Indian Ocean, and to remove the mists
which overhang the highly interesting Bahari-Ngo.

From the time when Captain Speke left the Asua
his life is public. From Alexandria he telegram'd,
in April, 1863, to the Foreign Office, these " preg-
nant words : "—" Inform Sir Roderick Murchison
that all is well, that we are in lat. 14° 30' upon the
Nile, and that the Nile is settled." (See *Proceedings of the Royal Geographical Society*, vol. viii.,
No. III., p. 19 ; also " Annual Address " of May
25, 1863, *Proceedings*, vol. viii. No. IV.) The
startling assertion announced to the meeting of May
11, 1863, caused a prodigious sensation. Meanwhile Captain Speke was fêted in Egypt by His
Highness the Pasha, and by His Majesty of Pied-

mont was presented with a medal bearing the
gratifying inscription, "Honor est a Nilo." At
Southampton he was received by the civic authorities and sundry supporters, including a Colonel
Rigby,* of the Bombay army, ex-Consul of Zanzibar, who had taken a peculiar part in promoting,
for purely private reasons, the proposed Nyanza-Nile
expedition of Captain Speke *versus* the Mombas-Nile
exploration proposed by myself. On June 22nd,
1863, he received an ovation in the shape of a
special meeting of the Royal Geographical Society, when the windows were broken in by the
eager crowd, who witnessed, it is said, a somewhat
disenchanting exhibition.

From that day the fate of the "settlement" of the
Nile was well-nigh settled. Those who had hailed
the solution of the great problem with the highest
gratification, and who were most ready to accept it,
felt a sensible cooling of their enthusiasm. Despite

* " Ah ! that harsh voice, that arrogant style, that saucy super-
ficiality which decided on everything, that insolent arrogance that
contradicted everybody : it was impossible to mistake them ! And
Coningsby had the pleasure of seeing reproduced before him the
guardian of his youth * * * Nicholas *Rigby*." Chap. 11.

the differences which had sprung up between us, I
had been one of the first to pronounce the most
flattering opinion of the exploratory results, when
the first personal account of the chief explorer at
once showed me how little had been effected, compared with the enormous claims put forth. It is
something to pass over 350 untrodden miles: it is
something more to " settle the great Nile problem
for ever."

Forthwith controversies touching lake-issues and
other geographical points appeared in the public
papers. Captain Speke attempted to veto such
expressions of thought—so likely in this land !—
and " a welcome to Captain Speke " was put forth
in August, 1863, by *Blackwood's Magazine*—a
periodical from which, for reasons best known to
myself, and wholly unworthy of being placed before
the public, I have never of late years expected to
receive justice.* In January, 1864, the subject
was thrown open by Captain Speke's *Journal of*

---

* The author of the " Welcome"—written of course by way of
advertisement—boasted thus : " We were the first to satisfy ourselves with Captain Speke's geographical views." I congratulate the
Editors, and only hope that they will be the last.

the Discovery of the Source of the Nile. It went off rapidly for a short time, after which, despite all exertions on the part of the enterprising publishers, it suddenly ceased to make its way—thus dealing a second heavy blow to the "settlement" question. The last—the *coup de grace*—was the injudicious reproduction by Messrs. Blackwood of another volume, *What led to the Discovery of the Source of the Nile*, when nearly all Europe had made up its mind that "Non-Discovery" would be the more fitting term, and that "Sources," not "Source," would be the proper number. The book fell still-born from the press. It was a mere reprint, as is partially owned in the "Advertisement," of papers contributed to *Blackwood's Magazine* in 1859, 1860, when I first understood the danger to which I had exposed myself by not travelling alone, a lake seen only for 20-22 miles at the southern edge, and pro-longed by mere guesswork 240 miles to the north —reaching, in fact, N. lat. 2°, a country well known by report—sufficed to stultify the whole expedition. How publishers were found for it still passes my comprehension. This second book, without correct-ing a single error, offered only the insertion of notes

and passages upon a subject which we had both
tacitly agreed to avoid.

For nearly a year and a half—between June, 1863,
and November, 1864—Captain Speke's views touching the Nile Basin and the Nile Sources have been
before the world. I have hitherto avoided noticing
any of his statements, except in my absolutely necessary reply to a note addressed by him on January
14th, 1864, to the editor of the *Athenæum*. Had
we met at Bath the discussion which would have
resulted must have brought forth a far more searching scrutiny as regards the late expedition than can
now be expected. As it is, I must be dumb upon
many points, of which, under other circumstances, I
had a right to speak.

A glance at the Ptolomeian map appended to this
paper, and taken from Dr. Beke's lecture, alluded
to in the following pages, shows the scanty justice
with which the great Pelusiot has lately been termed
a "hypothetical humbug." The grand Divisio Aqua-
rum between the Nilotic Basin draining to the Mediterranean, and the Zambezian Basin discharging
into the Indian Ocean, is placed by Ptolemy in S.
at. 12° 30′. During the last year the Zambezi

expedition has brought home good geographical
and physical reasons,* which will be presently
adduced, for placing it in S. lat. 9°, when, a few
years ago, the boldest theorists hesitated to admit
the possibility of the Nile sources being derived
from S. lat. 3°. On the other hand the confluence
of the effluents from the eastern and western lake
reservoirs which form the true White or Œthiopian
Nile are placed by Ptolemy in N. lat. 2° 0′ 0″. A
reference to Captain Speke's map places the same
point where the Asua, Tubiri, or East Nile branch,
joins the western effluent from the Tanganyika Lake
and the Luta Nzige in N. lat. 3° 34′ 33″; and M.
Miani, it will be remembered, prolongs it 2° N.,
making a close approach to where (says Ptolemy)
" the River Nile becomes one, by the uniting of the
rivers that flow out of the two lakes which are
placed higher up." In this we have more than
coincidence. Like the White Nile, the Astapus,

* I say geographical and physical, meaning the results of
exploration. Before their return Dr. Beke had theoretically
inferred that, " if it were allowable to attempt to be definite in
a matter which is necessarily indefinite " (no European having
even then visited it), the division between the Mediterranean and
Indian Ocean waters " might be placed in 9° S. lat. and 27° E.
long."—*Westminster Review*, April, 1864, p. 327.

Blue River, or Nile of Bruce, passes through a lake, the Coloe Palus, which all identify with Lake Tsana. As is found in the lake reservoirs of the Œthiopian or True Nile, it is placed too far south, upon the equator, when it lies in N. lat. 12°. In the following pages I have attempted to show how this misconception may be accounted for.

After so long a silence upon the subject I am, methinks, justified in drawing public attention to what was effected by the expedition of 1857—59, which was under my almost unaided direction.* When wholly ignorant of the country, its language and trade, its manners and customs, preceded only by a French naval officer, who was murdered shortly after he landed on the coast, and but feebly supported by my late lamented friend Lieutenant-Colonel Hamerton, Her Majesty's Consul at Zanzibar, whom nearing death prevented from carrying out the best of intentions, I led the most disorderly of caravans into the heart of Eastern Africa, and discovered the Tanganyika and the Nyanza lakes.†

* In his *What led to the Discovery of the Source of the Nile*, (p. 298), Captain Speke maintains that his first sight of the " Ukerewe Sea " was " *the* discovery of the source of the Nile."

† Captain Speke chose again to employ Shaykh Said, my Ka-

I brought home sufficient information to smooth the path for all who chose to follow me. They had but to read the *Lake Regions of Central Africa* and volume xxx. of the Royal Geographical Society to learn what beads, what wires, what clothes are necessary, what guides, escort and porters are wanted, what facilities offer themselves, and what obstacles are to be expected. Dr. Beke has kindly found " reason to call this emphatically a memorable expedition." Except by a few esteemed friends it has hitherto either been ignored or forgotten.

The labours of the first expedition rendered the road easy for the second. The line had been opened by me to Englishmen, and they had but to tread in my steps. In the preceding pages I have shown how a thorough misconception of the Nile sources and a preoccupation of ideas prevented anything like a successful and a satisfactory exploration being as yet effected by those who succeeded me. The reader

filah-bashi, or caravan leader, and had to leave him behind at Kazeh. Baron von der Decken took my one-eyed Jemadar, and failed to reach the Nyassa or Southern Lake. Late communications from Zanzibar show that the " faithfuls " of the last expedition, who included some of the most objectionable of the first, have been ever since their return in the completest state of demoralisation.

must not, however, suppose—the mistake should be averted at the danger of iteration—that any charge of wilful misrepresenting, of asserting what he did not in every way believe, is brought against Captain Speke. When he declared in his "Taunton Speech" (December 24th, 1863) that as the real discoverer he "had in 1857 hit the Nile on the head, and in 1863 drove it down to the Mediterranean," he believed these words as firmly and as unreasoningly as he did in his "Victoria Nyanza" Lake. His peculiar idiosyncrasy of long brooding over thoughts and memories, secreting them until some sudden impulse brought them forth, may explain this great improbability. His mind, moreover, could not grasp a fact, else how explain his "partial eclipse of the moon on the 5th *and* 6th of January, 1863" (*Journal*, p. 243). Nor does he know the use of words. "A village built on the most luxurious principles" is a mass of dirty huts; a "king of kings" is a petty chief; a "splendid court" is a display of savagery; and the "French of those parts" are barbarians somewhat superior to their neighbours. "Nelson's *monument* at *Charing Cross*" is a specimen of what we may expect in

Central Africa. I cannot but regret that, in one point at least, his example should hitherto have been followed by his last companion. Captain Grant has not (I refer to his printed paper " on the Native Tribes visited by Captains Speke and Grant in Equatorial Africa," read before the Ethnological Society, June 30, 1863) owned the vast benefits which the second derived from the first expedition.*

I must here express my gratitude to Messrs. Beke, Vaux, and Hogg for the perusal of the valuable papers which are mentioned in the follow pages, and by which my case has been so much strengthened. To Doctors Livingstone and Kirk, and to Messrs Findlay† and Bates, Fellow and Assistant Secretary of the Royal Geographical Society, my best thanks are also due in carrying out conclusions

* The paper opens with " dividing the country traversed into districts," and the descriptions of the eastern and southern districts are borrowed almost literally from my writings, without a word of acknowledgment, even to say that I took any part in " Captain Speke's previous journey."

† When last in Western Africa I received a letter from Mr. Findlay, drawing my attention to the northern watershed of the Tanganyika, and suggesting a great part of what is said in these pages.

for which no one is answerable but myself. And I here also record my obligation to Mr. Trelawney Saunders of Messrs. E. Stanford and Co.'s firm : he has not only drawn my sketch-map, but also, by his extensive and accurate study, he has been enabled to draw it correctly.

To the veteran African geographer, Mr. James Macqueen, my thanks are especially due for permission to reprint his valuable and original letters on "Captain Speke's Discovery of the Source of the Nile." His literary labours in the cause of the Dark Peninsula have extended through half a century, and hardly ever before has he shown greater acumen or higher spirit—to say nothing of his inimitable dryness of style—than in those compositions, put forth at a time when the English world was bowing down before their latest idol. Mr. James Grant, who first ushered them into existence, has also obligingly allowed me to present them to the public in a connected form.

LAKE TANGANYIKA,

PTOLEMY'S WESTERN LAKE-RESERVOIR OF THE NILE.

THE intelligence lately brought home by Dr. Livingstone and his scientific co-operator, Dr. Kirk, throws a remarkable light upon a hitherto dark question. It verifies in a striking way a detail of Ptolomeian geography, until now either ignored or accounted for by an error of copyists. I allude to the northern drainage of the Tanganyika Lake, and to the southern limit of the great Nilotic basin, as far as the latter is at present known.

In a letter from Dr. Livingstone, read at the meeting of the Royal Geographical Society, June 13, 1864, occurs this highly interesting statement :—

' With regard to the existence of a large river flowing into the northern end of Nyassa from Tanganyika, Dr. Livingstone was assured by all the natives of whom he inquired that there was no such stream, but that two small rivers alone enter the lake from the north. The numerous streams met with on this journey (viz., the last in 1863) flowing from the west seem to warrant the conclusion that no flow of water from Tanganyika is necessary to account for the great depth of the (Nyassa) lake and the perennial flow of the Shiré.'

Dr. Kirk, who makes the Nyassa Water 200 miles long by 15 to 60 broad, stated personally at the same meeting :—

'As to a river coming in from the north, the only ones we heard of were two small ones ; one named in a generic way the Rovu, which simply means "river," and the other, which they describe as a small river coming in from a marsh.'

Since that time, Dr. Kirk kindly placed in my hands, with permission to publish, the following valuable note :—

'The region between the Nyassa and Tanganyika Lakes, being as yet unexplored, our knowledge of the animals inhabiting these waters becomes of some interest in guiding us to a solution of the vexed question as to their continuity or their separation.

On the former supposition the Tanganyika must belong to the Zambezi hydrographic basin, otherwise it will pass to the Congo* or the Nile.

'When the Tanganyika was discovered, a collection of its shells was formed by Capt. Burton; the same has been done on the shores of the Nyassa by myself. Between these there is *no* community of species, while both contain many new forms.

' Among those from the Nyassa is one of a type for the first time observed in Africa; being large and handsome, it could not easily be overlooked were it present in the Tanganyika.

' On the other hand, Capt. Burton's collection possesses one allied to a species common on the Nile, and unknown on the Nyassa. This favours my opinion that no communication exists between the two waters.†

* My visit to the rapids of the Congo River in August and September, 1863, convinced me that the north-eastern or smaller fork of that great river issues from an equatorial lake unconnected with the Tanganyika. At this moment it may have been visited by my enterprising friend Paul du Chaillu, who has proposed for himself the noble task of penetrating to the Nile Basin from Western Africa.

† Dr. Kirk, a naturalist, and a man full of facts, attaches some weight to community of forms arguing continuity of water. Others deny the inference.

' We now know that the fish of the Nyassa Lake
are peculiar to itself, and differ from those of the
Lower Shiré, its outlying stream, which is isolated
from the upper part by a formidable series of falls
and rapids. Of the fish of the Tanganyika nothing is
known, otherwise this geographical question might
be almost set at rest.

' The wide distribution of animals and plants over
Tropical Africa is in strong contrast to the very
local and peculiar nature of the fauna of its great
fresh-water lakes.

(Signed) ' J. Kirk.'

Dr. Livingstone has also favoured me with the
details concerning a weed from which the accolents
of the Nyassa extract their salt. That great traveller
wrote :—'I thought that I had a specimen of the plant
which floats ashore at Lake Nyassa, and from which
the natives obtain a salt used in cooking, but I cannot
find it. When chewed its taste is distinctly salt. If
so used in Lake Tanganyika, it may account for the
freshness, though I confess I feel more inclined to
the theory of an outlet still unknown.' This remarkable lacustrine production is wanting to the Tan-

ganyika water, and its adjacent tribes are obliged to transport the condiment from various diggings lying at considerable distances.   Dr. Kirk has thus explained the matter :—

' Understanding now your question, I may attempt a reply.

' The weed gathered and burned, whose ashes serve as a relish to food for the Nyassa natives, is the " *Potamogeton pectinatus* " of Linnæus.   With this is often mingled small quantities, perhaps accidentally, of *Valisneria spiralis*.   Where salt is plenty, I have never known this used.

' Salt is washed at the south end of the Nyassa, and carried up its western bank for sale.   It was a good way up the western shore, and at a distance from any salt-washings, where I saw the weed collected.

(Signed)   'J. KIRK.'

Thus, it is evident there is no connection between the Tanganyika and the Nyassa reservoirs.   What then, I would inquire, becomes of the surplus water from the Tanganyika Lake ?

In company with the lamented Captain Speke I

explored, in February, 1858, the great basin since identified by Mr. Hogg with the "Zambre" or "Zambere" of old geographers.* We dwelt on its eastern borders till May 25, visiting (April 26) Uvira, our farthest northerly point, about 10 or 12 miles from the end of the lake. There my hopes of discovering the Nile Sources were rudely dashed to the ground. Receiving a visit from the three stalwart sons of the local sultan, Maruta, the subject of the mysterious stream which all my informants, Arab as well as African, had made to issue from the Tanganyika, and which for months we had looked upon as the Western Head-Stream of the Nile, was at once brought forward. All declared (probably falsely) that they had visited it; all asserted that the Rusizi River enters into, instead of flowing from, the Tanganyika. I felt sick at heart. The African's account of stream-direction is often diametrically opposed to fact: seldom the Arab's; in this point I differ totally from Captain Speke. But

* P. 4 of a learned paper, " On some old maps of Africa in which the Central Equatorial Lakes are laid down nearly in their true position." From the *Transactions of the Royal Society of Literature*, vol. viii., new series.

our unruly crew of the Wajiji savages would not suffer us to remain at Uvira, much less to penetrate northwards. We were therefore compelled to return hurriedly, and thus, as I have related (*Lake Regions of Central Africa*, vol. ii., p. 117), the problem was fated to remain a mystery.*

Respecting the Southern Tanganyika, the Arabs of Kazeh, who have frequently and in large parties visited the lands of the Marungu lying at the extremity which faces Nyassa, positively informed me (*loc. cit.*, p. 153) that the " Runangwa or Marungu River, which drains the southern countries towards the Tanganyika, equals the Malagarazi (or eastern feeder of that lake) in volume ; " and all agreed in making it an influent, not an effluent. Had there been an important stream in that direction, the colony of Arab merchants which, for several years, has inhabited Lusenda or Usenda,† capital of the Cazembe, lying

---

* I distinctly deny that any " misleading by my instructions from the Royal Geographical Society as to the position of the White Nile," left me unconscious of the vast importance of ascertaining the Rusizi River's direction. The fact is, Captain Speke was deaf and almost blind, I was paralytic, and we were both helpless. We did our best to reach it, and we failed.

† First visited by Dr. de Lacerda e Almeida, in 1798. Generally

to the south-west of the Tanganyika Lake, would soon have found their way northwards. The same consideration renders Mr. Cooley's obsolete and obstinate confusion of three Lakes into one a moral impossibility. Another impossibility may be observed in the Mombas Mission's map, which has also confounded the three Lakes. The water is made so broad, that no native canoe would attempt to cross it. They must be first supplied with sextants, or at least with mariners' compasses. But Mr. Cooley still fights fiercely for his own misbegotten confusion ; the missionaries have given up theirs. Like a navigable river in Arabia, such a water-way, 800 miles in length, would have altered the state of the whole African interior.

Returning to England in May, 1859, I found geographers unwilling to believe that a reservoir 250 to 300 miles long, and situated at a considerable altitude in the African zone of almost constant rain, can maintain its level without efflux. Moreover, they argued that the freshness of the water would, under normal circumstances, prove the escape of

placed about S. lat. 8° 10' and E. long. 29°. Of late years many Arabs and Sawahilis have " squatted " there.

saline substances washed down by tributaries from the area of drainage.

The *Journal of the Royal Geographical Society* (vol. xxx., 1860) lost no time in offering a solution of the " strange hydrological puzzle." Earl de Grey and Ripon's address thus enters upon the question : —" The configuration of the country to the north- ward (of the Tanganyika) gives us excellent reason to believe that the northern tributary is correctly described; but whether the river mentioned as *entering* the lake at the south does not really run *out of it*, is a fair matter for discussion." * The visits of Dr. Livingstone to the Shirwa and Nyassa Lakes, then not thoroughly explored—the circumstance that the three waters, Tanganyika, Nyassa, and Shirwa, were approximately at the same level †—and the possibility that the Tanganyika might be the highest of them all, afforded a satis-

---

* The theory is usually attributed to Mr. Francis Galton, F.R.G.S. ; and as long as Captain Speke's " Lunæ Montes," as he loved to call them, were allowed to blockade the north of Tanga- nyika, it was exceedingly plausible.

† Captain Speke had placed the Tanganyika at 1844 feet above the sea. Dr. Livingstone gave 2000 feet of altitude to the Shirwa : difference, 156 feet.

factory hypothetical solution. The connection, with or without small intermediate waters, between the Tanganyika and the Nyassa, would account for the surplus waters of the former, and for the non-variation of height in the splendid Shiré River which drains the latter.

On the other hand, Captain Speke, shortly after our return, published, much against my wish, two papers in *Blackwood's Edinburgh Magazine*, September and October, 1859. They were accompanied by a sketch-map, in which, to my astonishment, appeared, for the first time in print, a huge range estimated to rise 6000 or 8000 feet, and dubbed the "Mountains of the Moon." At first the segment of a circle, it gradually shaped itself into a colt's foot or a Lord Chancellor's wig, and it very effectually cut off all access from the Tanganyika to the Nile. Without recalling to mind things that should be now forgotten, I must record my unceasing struggle against the introduction of a feature which was frequently copied into popular maps abroad and at home.* All that Captain Speke could say of the

* "We find in the centre of Africa a high group of hills surrounding the head of the Tanganyika Lake, composed chiefly of

Lunar Horseshoe was explained in our Journal (vol. xxxiii.). " Both the Arabs and the natives said the Rusizi (at the northern end) was a very large river, much greater than the Malagarazi River .... for which reason I imagined the mountains encircling the head of the Tanganyika must necessarily attain an altitude of from 8000 to 10,000 feet." * These heights, as Mr. Findlay the learned Editor of Volume xxxiii. remarks, were " not shown in Captain Speke's map of the route sent home after the visit to the Tanganyika head ; nor in his sketch-

argillaceous sandstones, which I suppose to be the Lunæ Montes (!) of Ptolemy, or the Soma Giri of the ancient Hindus " (? ?).   (Captain Speke's *Journal of the Discovery of the Source of the Nile,* Introduc. p. xv.)   In p. 263, he owns to having built up these mountains " solely on scientific geographical reasonings," and he actually falls into the venerable error of deriving from almost the same source the Nile, the Congo, and the Zambezi.   In a letter read before the Royal Geographical Society (Nov. 14, 1864), Captain Grant, if I rightly understood him, asserted that the mountains were the work of the engraver, and that Captain Speke was amused by the exaggeration.   But Captain Grant should have visited the map-room of the Royal Geographical Society, where he would have found a map by Captain Speke showing the Lunar Horseshoe in all its hideousness.   Mr. Findlay, F.R.G.S., has another.

* Captain Speke's " View of Mount Mfumbiro " (*Journal,* p. 214), which he believes to reach 10,000 feet, shows a cone of 4000 at most.

map sent in July, 1858. It was impossible to see them on either journey. In the first expedition the alleged north point was not approached within 160 miles, and the formation of the head of the lake prevented distant view in any direction. During the second exploration the nearest and highest point, the Mfumbiro Cone, raised to 10,000 feet, supposed to have been 50 miles distant, and the centre of the range is marked as 150 miles from the nearest point of the route." In Captain Speke's original map, sent from Egypt to the Royal Geographical Society, and published by Mr. E. Stanford, June, 1863, this moon-shaped range is not laid down; the name is given to two parallel sierras flanking the northern end of the Tanganyika, and far south of the position attributed to the Mountains of the Moon in his later map.* The objectionable feature was, after three or four years, duly rejected.

During his last march, Captain Speke apparently coincided with Earl de Grey's Address, using these

* Says Mr. Hogg (p. 38), "In the map published by Mr. Edward Stanford, June 22, 1863, and signed by Captain Speke, ' 26 February, 1863,' the mountains termed by that traveller the ' Mountains of the Moon ' are placed at the north extremity of Lake Tanganyika ; but in his own map, published in his Journal in

words (vol. xxxiii. p. 324): "It was a pity I did not change the course I gave to the Marungu River (*i.e.*, making it an effluent not an influent), but I forgot my lesson and omitted to do so." In his *Journal* (p. 90), he thus expresses himself—"Ever perplexed about the Tanganyika being a still lake, I inquired of Mohinna and other old friends what they thought about the Marungu River (at its southern extremity); did it run into or out of the lake? And they all still adhered to its running *into* the lake, which is the *most conclusive argument* that it does run *out* of the lake." A truly extraordinary train of reasoning!

Presently it became evident to every geographer who cast his eye upon the map produced by the Nile Expedition of 1860-1863, that the Rusizi River might drain the Tanganyika Lake either into the water called the Luta Nzigé—Dead Locust—or by some other means into the White River, the Nile. Many years ago Mr. Macqueen received from an Arab

December last, Captain Speke in the construction of it has altered their position and inserted them around the west and north sides of the more northern Lake Rusizi (*N.B. manifestly a widening of the river*), and has also given them a certain mythical colt's foot form."

who had visited Unyamwezi, the following remarkable statement, touching the Tanganyika:—"It is well known by all the people there, that the river which goes through Egypt takes its source and origin from the Lake." (*Journal, Royal Geographical Society,* vol. xv. pp., 371—374.) Captain Speke, on return from his first journey, thus recorded the information given by Shaykh Hamed, a respectable Arab trader: —" A large river called Marungu supplies the lake (Tanganyika) at its southern extremity; but except that and the Malagarazi River on the eastern shore, none of any considerable size pour their waters into the lake. But, on a visit to the northern end, *I saw one*, which was very much larger than either of them, and *which I am certain flowed out of the lake;* for, although I did not venture on it, in consequence of its banks being occupied by desperately savage negroes, inimical to strangers, *I went so near its outlet that I could see and feel the outward drift of the water.*"—(*Blackwood*, Sept., 1859, and Captain Speke's *What led to the Discovery of the Source of the Nile*, p. 20. N.B. The italics are my own.) Several authors have recently recorded their adherence to this opinion. My learned friend Mr. W.

S. W. Vaux, *On the Knowledge the Ancients possessed of the Sources of the Nile* (from the *Transactions of the Royal Society of Literature*, vol. viii.
New Series, p. 29), thus expresses himself:—" I
cannot myself help thinking that this Luta Nzigé
will be ultimately found to be one of a chain of
lakes of which the Tanganyika is the largest and
most southern; the more so, as I have already
stated I feel no confidence in the emplacement of
Captain Speke's "Mountains of the Moon," which, on
his map at least, would bar any outlet from the
southern to the northern lake." Others have hypo-
thesized a gorge or valley by which the Tanganyika
waters might flow northwards through the " Colt's-
foot Range," which has, I have said, now been
abolished. Mr. John Hogg (*loc. cit.*, p. 23) refers
to his Plate III., a map published in 1623 by the
most distinguished geographer of his age, Gerhard
Kauffmann, who is better known by his Latin name
of *Mercator*, he having been the inventor of the
geographical *Projection* called after him. " In this
system ' Nilus fl.,' as Ptolemy believed, derives his
western fork from an immense water named Zaire
or Zembre Lacus, and corresponding with our Tan-

ganyika. The eastern arm issues from ' Zaflan
Lacus,' the *Zambesi* of some authors, and corre-
sponds with the lake now called Maravi or Nyassa.
Another branch of the ' Nilus,' at about 1° south of
the Equator, flows from a smaller nameless lake, at
the northern extremity of which is a place called
' Garava.'" Mr. Hogg suggests this to be a cor-
ruption of " Ukewere," meaning in the local tongue
Island-land. Finally, the south-easternmost feeder
proceeds from a lake, "the *Barcena*, which is doubtless meant for the Baringa, for the word may also
be written Barenca or *Barenga*." It is clearly the
Bahari-Ngo, the " Great Sea or Water," yet unexplored, and placed in our maps as the " Baringo."
Dr. Beke, the traveller who deserves all praise for
suggesting a feasible way to explore the Nile basin,
quotes De Barros:—" The Nile has its origin in a
great lake (the Tanganyika), and after traversing
many miles northwards it enters a very large lake
which lies under the Equator." This would be
either the Bahr el Ghazal (probably the Nile of
Herodotus), or the Luta Nzigé; on the other hand,
the Portuguese travellers were fond of distorting
Ptolomeian geography. The same geographer, in

an admirable lecture lately printed,* thus records
his matured opinion :—"Whereas in the map inserted in the *Sources of the Nile*, I marked Tanganyika as being within the 'not impossible' limits
of the basin of the Nile, I am now inclined to place
this lake within the *probable* limits of that basin,
and to make it, in fact, the upper course of the
Giant River of Egypt."

An objection to the theory that the Tanganyika
Lake drains into the Luta Nzigé at once suggests
itself, and it would be fatal if reliance could be
placed upon it. I allude to the levels. Lake Tanganyika is allowed but 1844 feet. Captain Speke
(p. 332 of the *Journal of the Royal Geographical
Society*, vol. xxxiii.) argues that the Luta Nzigé is
2161 feet, or upwards of 300 feet above the Tanganyika. But his boiling-point observation was made
at Paira, a station distant from the stream ; and even
to obtain that altitude he was obliged to add the
mean of certain differences amounting to 368 feet;
this emendation is generally rejected by geographers.

* *On the Sources of the Nile*, &c., &c., delivered in the Theatre
of the London Institution, January 30, 1864, by Charles T. Beke,
Esq., Phil. D., F.S.A.

During our exploration of Tanganyika the state of our vision would, I am convinced, explain a greater difference than the fraction of a degree. Without reference to variation of barometric pressure, our thermometer had altered from first to last 1° (F.) = 535 feet. On our return, after the first expedition, to Konduchi, a harbour on the East African coast, our B. P. thermometer (a "bath" or common wooden instrument) boiled at 214° (F.). This would give a difference of about 1000 feet. The Nyanza water was made 3550 feet high by the first expedition. The second raised it to 3745, and made it drain by the Luchuro or Kitangule River, "Little Lake Windermere," which being placed at a figure of 3639, thus runs 106 feet up hill. It may also be observed that whilst the "Ripon Falls," a mere salmon-leap 12 feet high, are placed at 3308 feet above sea-level, the "Victoria Nyanza" rises 3740. Either, then, the surface of the supposed lake shows a difference in level of 432, or there are two lakes, or the levels are worthless.

I adduce these cases out of many, to show how unreliable are such approximations of altitude. It is, however, gratifying to find that Captain Speke places Gondókoro, which some have raised to 1600 and 1900 feet, at a figure of 1298, whilst Mr. Consul Petherick (February 25, 1863) reduced it by a mean of three observations to 1265. Assuming Gondó-koro, about 5° N. lat., to be even 1600 feet above sea-level, we still have from the head of the Tangan-yika Lake, in 3° S. lat. (8° × 60° = 480 direct miles), a fall of 244 feet, almost exactly six inches per mile. Captain Speke's and Mr. Petherick's ob-servations would give 550 feet, or one foot and two inches per mile—an ample inclination.* Moreover, the Luta Nzigé is theoretically placed 1000 to 1200 feet lower than the Nyanza Lake, that is to say, between 2350 and 2550 feet above sea-level, and the altitude has been further reduced to 2250.

But truth to say, very little fall is required for the 200 miles separating the Tanganyika and the Luta Nzigé, and the want of inclination may explain the marshiness of " the sort of backwater to the great river." A correspondent of the *Morning Advertiser* (March 22, 1864), known to be the African geo-

---

* Dr. Beke, *The Sources of the Nile*, pp. 30, 36, calculates the fall of the main stream, as high up as then known to him, to be less than one foot per mile throughout.

grapher, Mr. Macqueen, remarks of the Dead Locust Lake, " At this point should commence the supposed backwater of 166 miles in length towards the S.S.W. But how are we to arrange the subsequent descent of the river beyond the northern point of this lake? To the point where the river is met with beyond Paira, 120 miles from the Karuma Falls, the descent is stated to be 1000 feet (say 400 feet higher than Gondókoro), and consequently 300 feet below the level of the north point of the Luta Lake. How, then, could the Nile form a backwater for this? This is not thought of, nor explained. The fact is, that this backwater expanse was, we believe, made out in London in order to cobble something like consistency and unity, and also to account for the diminution of the river in magnitude, which they found as they advanced northwards." Dr. Beke (loc. cit., p. 25), on the other hand, observes that " Captain Speke adopted the conjecture of Dr. Murie, whom he met in Gondókoro." This " backwater " enabled him to explain how, with a fall of 2·5 feet per mile, the waters of the river occupied 86 days in flowing down 200 geographical miles—in other words, 2·25 miles in 24 hours.

Thus, by draining the Tanganyika so as to maintain its surface at an almost constant level, the meaningless backwater would resolve itself into a link in the lake chain, the *Nili Paludes* of the ancients, usually placed in N. lat. 5°. They are called *immensas paludes*,* a title which they deserve better than the No, Nuvier, or Bahr el Ghazal. In Seneca's account of the contemporary journey made by the two centurions despatched by Nero *ad investigandum caput Nili*, about 70 years before Ptolemy's day, we find that they travelled 800 to 890 Roman miles from the well-known station, Meroe; that is to say, reaching N. lat. 3° or 4° (*Nat. Quæst.* lib. vi. chap. 8). The two rocks from which the vast force of the water broke forth is a feature remaining to be described; it may allude to a rapid at the southern extremity of the Luta Nzigé.†

* Why this water, being 160 to 180 miles long, should be called the *Little* Luta Nzigé, and where the Great one is, I am at a loss to determine.

† At the cataracts of Makedo, M. De Bono learned from the natives that the river fell some nine perpendicular feet, and that four or five days south of these falls it rose from an immense lake, into whose other extremity a river fell. M. Lejean at first conjectured this to be the Nyanza. After the second expedition he pro-

The principal alterations which I would introduce into the map appended to Captain Speke's paper (vol. xxxiii. *Journal of the Royal Geographical Society*) are as follows:—

1. Draining Lake Tanganyika into the Luta Nzigé.

2. Converting the Nyanza into at least a double lake, the northern part fed by rivers from the western highlands, and the southern by small streams from the south to the south-east. The former in Captain Speke's book appears to be merely a broadening of some large river, and thus only can we explain the phenomenon of six outlets in 30 geographical miles. * He was no

posed the Luta Nzigé, lying between the Equator and N. lat. 3°. (Bulletin de la Société de Géographie. Cinquième Série, tome vi.)

In Captain Speke's Journal (p. 466) we find that the Waganda still call the "Ripon Falls" *stones*.

* Within a distance of 1° the map shows three first-rate streams, viz., the Mwerango or Mwarango, the Luajerri, and the Napoleon Channel issuing from the Nyanza Lake. I believe this to be a physical impossibility, and the same is acknowledged by the Bulletin (p. 261). In p. 281 of his *Journal*, Capt. Speke was informed by "all the men of the country" that the Mwerango rose "in the hills to the southward," or came "from the lake;" and he adopted the latter because it suited his preconceived opinions.

The *Westminster Review*, vol. xxv. p. 315, New Series,

linguist, and we find in his *Journal* that the word Nyanza may mean the "Great Victoria Nyanza" Lake, "a pond in the palace" (p. 324), "a piece of water, whether a pond, river, or lake" (p. 389), or "the Nile." It will be remembered that during his third expedition Captain Speke, instead of striking, as before, the south of the lake and coasting or marching along it, nowhere sighted the Nyanza waters till he reached Mashonde, about 50 miles south of the Equator, leaving wholly unnoticed 2° 15′ (= 135 miles) between the spot where he struck the lake during the first expedition. Yet when returned to England he rejected the normal dotted line which shows uncertainty, and inserted in his own map the normal survey line, which was not adopted in the *Journal of the Royal Geographical Society.* The northern water was probably a widening of the great Kitangule River, a projection of the extensive Luchuro valley. We find (*Journal*, p. 469) that even in the moment of triumph the explorer asked himself if the

suggests that Capt. Speke, in assuming his "Victoria Nyanza" to be a single lake, was mistaken, just as were the Mombas missionaries with respect to their Ujiji, or Unyamwezi Lake. I had not read that excellent review when the above was written.

volume of the Kitangule River was not equal to that of "the Nile," and he answered the question in a very unsatisfactory way. He saw it at certain intervals as far eastward as the "Ripon Falls;" but the "spur of a hill" in Kira shut out his view of the outlet of Napoleon Channel. His actual inspection of the Nyanza, then, was about 50 out of 450 miles; all the rest was hearsay. He travelled in the conviction that "*the* lake" was on his right; but he never verified that conviction. When living with Rumanika of Karagwa, at some 60 direct miles from "*the* lake," he did not personally assure himself of its existence. The King of Uganda detained him two months in his palace without allowing him to see "*the* lake," distant a five hours' march. The offer made to him by King Mtesa, namely, to send him home in one month by a frequented route, doubtless through the Masai country on the east of Nyanza (p. 294), points to a direct road which can only be explained by the separation of the Nyanza into two or more waters.* So in p. 187 of Captain Speke's

* Captain Speke of course understood that his informants meant him to strike the north-eastern side of the "Great Lake" at "Uvuma" or some such part. But the Masai, as far as I

Journal, Irungu of Uganda expressed his surprise that the traveller had come all the way round to Uganda, when he could have taken the short, safe, and well-known route *viâ* Masai-land and Usoga, by which an Arab caravan had travelled. His words are, " He (Irungu) then told me he was surprised that I had come all the way round to Uganda, when the road by the Masai country was so much shorter." In p. 130 the petty chief Makaka assures Captain Speke that "there were two lakes and not one :" unfortunately the hearer understood that the Bahari-Ngo was alluded to. In p. 197 he mistakes the broad waters of the "Luero lo Urigi" for the Nyanza itself, and gives a fabulous account of how the former lake had "become a small swamp." In p. 428 Murondi, who had once travelled to the Masai frontier, said "It would take a month to go in boats from Kira to (the) Masai (country), where there is another Nyanza joined by a strait to the big Nyanza, which Mtesa's boats

know, inhabit part of the lands between Mombas and the south-eastern edge of the true Nyanza. They are bounded on the north by the Gallas, and are not a large tribe, being split into subtribes, as the Wakuafi. In Captain Speke's *Journal* map he assigns to them far too large a territory.

frequent for salt; but the same distance could be accomplished in four days overland and three days afterwards by boat." This suggests a very different form of coast line and country from that shown in Captain Speke's map. In p. 333 he hears from "Kidi officers" of a high mountain behind the Asua River, and a lake navigated by the Galla "inhabitants" in very large vessels; but he never investigates the report.

In the *Journal* there are many contradictions, to be reconciled only by supposing the upper "Victoria Nyanza Lake" to consist of sundry lagoons; and we may observe that nowhere in the cuts of the *Journal* (*e.g.*, p. 390) is a sea horizon shown. For instance, if the waterway be continuous, how is it that the Usoga defeated King Mtesa's army when a fleet of war canoes could have been sent? At Mtesa's court, Maribu, the officer sent to fetch Captain Grant, said he should *walk* (about half the way over hills and bad land) to the mouth of the Katonga influent, boat it to Sese Island, where the local King keeps all his large vessels, and be at Kitangule (River) in a very short time (p. 317). Why should he walk if there was a way by water?

On the north-west of the lake the "numerous islands" of the Royal Geographical Society's *Journal* (omitted in Captain Speke's *Journal* map) seem to be a bungling explanation of a plurality of waters thrown into one. The group called Sese, *forty* in number, or *one* (p. 399), placed (p. 276) opposite Kituntu, off the mouth of the Katonga River, and where the Uganda King keeps one of his canoe fleets, was admitted into the explorer's sketch-map, but omitted by our *Journal*. The Kitiri Island (*Blackwood*, Sept. 1859), which reappeared, mentally, to Captain Speke on the way to Usoga (*Journal of the Discovery*, p. 399), and the reefs and shoals (have the Waganda words for these fine distinctions?), may be, like Ukerewe and Mazita, a mere peninsula. We have another mysterious island, in which Mgussa the African Neptune, dwells. There is again another island in the Nyanza, to which Captain Speke banished his recreant followers (p. 492). Lastly, in Captain Speke's *Journal* map the south-eastern shore is "studded with islands" derived from "Arab information." Project these "islands," let them meet in the middle of the "Great Victoria Nyanza," and something like the real shape of that preposterous feature will, I believe, be obtained.

3. Detaching the Bahari-Ngo from the Nyanza waters. This reservoir (the Baharingo of M. Leon d'Avanchers* and Mr. Missionary Erhardt, and vulgarly Baringo, as written by Mr. Missionary Krapf, who first heard of its existence) drains the mass of highlands between the Equator and 3° S. lat., and sends forth what M. Miani, the discoverer, calls Ascia or Acioà, Captain Grant the Aswa, and Captain Speke the Usua or Asua. I believe it to be the real White Nile, the so-called Nyanza effluents being of minor importance. "It is by no means improbable," says M. Vaux, "that we may hereafter discover, as Dr. Beke has urged more than once, *a* source of the Nile in a chain of mountains to the south-east of the lake Nyanza—a discovery which will confirm in a signal manner all the essential inferences he has deduced from his informants" (p. 24). In p. 598 of Captain Speke's *Journal* we are told that the Asua cannot issue from the Nyanza, "as its waters

* See Journal of the Royal Geographical Society, vol. xxx. p. 106. Mr. Macqueen there remarks, "M. Leon supposes this (Lake) to be the source of the Seboth (Sobat), but it is more probable that it is the main stream of the Nile."

were falling and not much discoloured." Yet in his map he derives it from the Bahari-Ngo, and connects the latter with the Nyanza, directly contradicting himself. Only by assuming the Asua to be the true White Nile, and to head in highlands, can we account for the snows of Æschylus (*Æthiopis Fragm.* 139, ed. Didot) and Ptolemy (τὰς χιόνας, lib. iv. chap 8) with which the Moon Mountain feeds the two Lake Reservoirs of the Nile, and for the express statements of Brun-Rollet and other travellers who ascended the stream, all of whom trace the Nile from the land of the Madi up to the mountains in the south-east. Thus, too, can we explain the Arab epithet " White " applied to the true Nile,* the colour

* The venerable priest Achoreus has still to prove his assertion
     Vana fides veterum, Nilo, quo crescat in arva
     Æthiopum prodesse nives.
The Bahr el Azrek, or Blue River, like the Rhone after issuing from the Lake of Geneva, the Tacazze, Bahr el Aswad, or Black River (Atbara, Astaboras of Ptolemy), so called from its dark earthy tinge during the rains. The Bahr el Abyaz, or White River, may point to glacier water: a mudd y stream can hardly issue from a lake. This was suggested to me in the year 1857 by Mr. Tyndall, who had long resided in Switzerland. In a lecture delivered before the Literary and Philosophical Society of Newcastle-upon-Tyne, Mr. Brayley expressed the opinion that " assuming snowy mountains to supply water to the Nyanza, that water must necessarily issue from glaciers: for, from the

of glacier water. Dr. Krapf also heard, when near Kenia, of a river running from the south-east and forming the head-waters of the Nile. Since my return from Zanzibar in 1860, I have never ceased to recommend a reconnaissance of the Nile *viâ* Mombas, where a march of 300 instead of 1100 miles through an easy country, at a far less cost than 7000*l.*, would give very different results from the " gigantic *ignis fatuus*" that has lately amazed the public, and has reminded thoughtful men of a similar statement, as ecstatically made some ninety years ago by Abyssinian Bruce, and as unreasonably received by the unscientific public.

Viewed in this light, how admirably exact in A.D. 136 was Ptolemy the Græco-Egyptian's description of this mysterious region. His " Αἰθίοπες Ἀνθρωποφάγοι," inhabiting the " Barbaric Gulf"—lands between Menuthias (Zanzibar) Island and the Mountain of the Moon (Kilima-njaro and its neighbours)— are the cannibal Wadoe. The melted snows have been discovered in Chhaga by Baron Carl von der

relative properties of fluid and solid water, it is impossible for a body of perpetual snow—that is to say, of snow at the lower limit of perpetual snow—to become a body of water, without first passing into the state of glacier-ice."—Dr. Beke (*loc. cit.*, p. 26).

Decken and his lamented companion Mr. Thornton, despite all the dicta of Mr. Cooley. The name "Mountain (chain) of the Moon" is manifestly a Greek translation or adaptation of Unyamwezi, which Mr. Cooley still insists upon corrupting to "*Monomoezi.*"

Ptolemy placed his chain in lat. 57° E. long. and 12° 30′ S. lat., extending latitudinally 10° (= 600 miles) to 67° E. long. The longitude, as Mr. Hogg very sensibly suggests, might have been computed from S. Antonio, and thus would answer to 30° and 40° east of Greenwich. This includes the icy highlands of Chhaga, and the mass of mountains, Mfumbiro, &c., to the west of the supposed Nyanza. I have treated this question at length in my *Lake Regions of Central Africa* (vol. ii. p. 178), and have not found reasons to alter my opinions. The older theory (see Macqueen's *Geographical Survey of Africa*, p. 240), which makes the Lunar Mountains extend from Camaroons in 3° 40′ N. lat., in an E. by N. and E.N.E. direction to Guardafui, has long since been abandoned.

As regards Ptolemy's latitudes, it must be remembered that he and his predecessor, Marinus of

Tyre (the Maury of antiquity), drew their information from the logs of traders who travelled on the eastern coast. He places the Prom. Aromatum, our Guardafui, in 6° N. lat., an error of 5° 48′ 50″ too far south, that well-known cape lying in 11° 48′ 50″. This misinformation touching a crucial station from which his departures down the East African coast are apparently calculated, would necessarily throw out his lower latitudes. Yet if the great water-parting be assumed to be at the head of the Marungu River, Ptolemy will have erred by only 2° 30′, making the position 12° 30′, instead of 9° —10° south. And as Dr. Beke (*loc. cit.*, p. 29) has remarked, "The recondite Jesuit, Athanasius Kircher, will be found right in substance, if not in form, when stating, as he does in his *Mundus Subterraneus* (vol. i. p. 72 *et seq.*), that in the Mountains of the Moon is the great Hydrophylacium of Africa, the central point of division between the waters flowing to the Mediterranean, to the Atlantic, and to the Indian Ocean." *

* Dr. Beke, as early as 1846—48, before the Snowy Alps of Eastern Africa, Kilima-njaro, and Kenia, were discovered, converted Ptolemy's longitudinal into a meridional range of Lunar Mountains. I cannot believe that the learned Pelusiot made

Ptolemy also places an Eastern lake in E. long. 65° and S. lat. 7°, and a Western in E. long. 57° and S. lat. 6°, which is nearly the centre of the Tanganyika Lake. It must not be forgotten that some geographers have represented Ptolemy's waters to be three: in one place (lib. iv. chap. 8) he speaks of them in the plural, αἱ τοῦ Νείλου λίμναι; in another (lib. iv. chap. 7) they are expressly stated to be two, δυὸ λιμνῶν.* But this might refer to the two largest in a Lake Region, where for years every traveller will discover some fresh lacustrine feature. Well may Mr. Hogg—following D'Anville—conclude: "It must, therefore, be acknowledged that these accounts of Ptolemy, which relate to the upper portion of the Nile and to the reservoir lakes beyond the Equator, to the head-streams of that mighty river, and to a range of mountains termed ' of the Moon,' from whence descend as well as from whose roots spring the waters and sources that feed those central lakes, *are in the main correct.*" I

any such mistake ; and I find between E. long. 30° and 40°, and from the Equator to S. lat. 5°, a mass of peaks and highlands forming a remarkable sierra.

* The Ptolemeian map in the " Margarita Philosophica " (A.D. 1503) shows three distinct " paludes Nili."

hold Ptolemy's Niger to be not less exactly laid
down than his Nile, and that he knew more about it
than Europe did before the days of Richard Lander.
And in confidence of his sagacity I cannot but
believe the Tanganyika to be the Western lake-
reservoir of Father Nile. The word "source" is
expressly avoided, in the belief, with Mr. Macqueen,
that a lake, unless it be a mere "eye" of water,
cannot be taken as the head of a river, though the
river may issue from it. "Lake Baikal is not the
head of the Yenessei River, Lake Tsana is not the
head of the Blue Nile, Lake Geneva is not the head
of the Rhone, Lake Lausanne is not the head of
the Rhine, Lake Superior is not the head of the
St. Lawrence, nor Lake Winnipeg the head of the
Saskatchewan; and so of other rivers on this
globe." *

I will conclude with a statement which to some
may appear paradoxical, namely, that the real
sources of the Nile—the "great Nile problem"—
so far from being "settled for ever" by the late
exploration, are thrown farther from discovery than
before. They are not, we have been told, *in*

* See also Dr. Beke (*loc. cit.*, p. 25).

nubibus, but they elude our vision.   The exploratory labours of years, perhaps of a whole generation, must be lavished before even a rough survey
of the southern Nilotic basin can treat the subject
with approximate correctness of detail.   " Mais les
sources du Nil, sont-elles découvertes ? " enquires
our fellow-labourer in the field of geographical
science, M. V. A. Malte Brun.   " *Nous ne le croyons
pas.*"   No geographar does, no geographer can, believe in the actual " settlement " of the Nile Sources.
That the Tanganyika is the Western " top head "
or reservoir—not *source*—of the Great Nile, and
that the Bahari-Ngo, which supplies the Tubiri, is
the Eastern, I have little doubt.   But the Arcanum
Magnum of Old-World Geography has not yet been
solved.   The venerable lines—

> " Arcanum Natura caput non prodidit ulli ;
>   Non licuit populis parvum te, Nile, videre,"

have gained rather than have lost significancy.   It
still remains to this generation, as to its forefathers,
" Caput quærere Nili "—to close the Canon of Geographical Discovery.

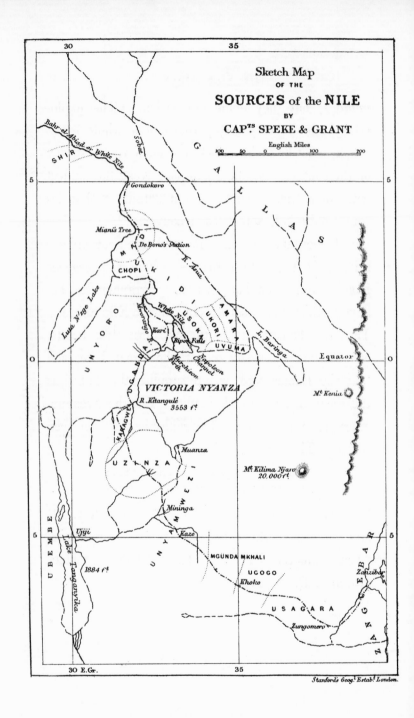

Sketch Map
OF THE
SOURCES of the NILE
BY
CAPTS. SPEKE & GRANT

English Miles

Stanford's Geog.l Estab.t London.

PART II.

CAPTAIN SPEKE'S DISCOVERY OF THE SOURCE OF THE NILE.

No. I.—INTRODUCTORY.

Towards the close of last summer, Captain Speke, with true Oriental authority,[*] announced that the source of the Nile was in the clouds, but forbade any one to attempt to seek out the particular point until *Blackwood* had told the world where that point was to be found. This remarkable announcement destroyed at once all claim to priority of discovery, because Homer told us 2500 years ago of the

" Stream of the Jove-descended Nile,"

which came from that sovereign's dominions amongst the clouds. Homer also tells us that Jupiter, with

[*] *Journal of the Discovery of the Source of the Nile.* By Captain Speke.—William Blackwood and Sons.

his licentious and profligate Olympian household train, yearly visited Upper Ethiopia, and spent twelve days in each visit in licentious revelry, drinking nectar, or the "pombe" of those remote regions. The actual point of Jove's sojourn in that quarter had to this day escaped the researches of mankind, until Captain Speke, amongst other strange discoveries and pictures made by him, has shown as clear as a pikestaff that it was in the capital of the kingdom of Uganda, then, as now, ruled by a King Mtesa, where licentiousness and profligacy prevail to an unlimited extent, and where the court and people do little else but prepare and drink "pombe," * "flirting" with ladies, and stealing queens' hearts, as Speke says they do. Amongst such Jupiter would readily find a kindred society, their revelries commencing then, as now, with "uproarious" banquets, and terminating with the fresh flowing

* POMBE.—This is a beverage made from the banana. It is a most delicious fruit, contains a large quantity of saccharine matter; and a drink or beer, when fermented and brewed from it, must be very strong. So delicious is the fruit, we verily believe that, if the gentlemen in Downing-street once tasted it, they would send Captain Speke to conquer Uganda to obtain it. Even Mr. Williams and the Chancellor of the Exchequer himself would vote an increase to the income tax to procure it.

cup to settle their squabbles. But of this country we shall have more to say by-and-by. In the meantime, we thank Captain Speke for deciding the above points along with his other discoveries, probably equally certain.

Blackwood having spoken out as strongly as its author dictated, we beings of the lower sphere, considering that the interdict has been removed, may now reverently and humbly approach the subject proclaimed by the same authority to be of the highest importance, and equally the property of all .kindreds and tongues, to examine calmly and minutely the narrative. Captain Speke can surely neither feel surprise nor take offence at such an examination. At the outset we must observe that it is Captain Speke only who speaks, and who tells us that he alone is qualified or to be allowed to speak on this subject; nay, he goes further, and says that no one will be allowed to dispute anything he has stated until they go to those distant parts and look at them with their own eyes! Till this is done, which will probably be some time, Captain Speke will enjoy his full triumph.

The work throughout is *Ego et Rex meus*, a

spirit which in our humble opinion confers neither credit nor respect upon the author or the work.

When we come to the geographical details of the great volume we will show how little remained unknown about the source of the Nile before Captain Speke ever thought of looking after it. In the meantime we observe that the publishers, Messrs. Blackwood and Sons, have, with their well-known abilities and resources, furnished us with a really good book, as a book—good paper, clear and legible type (a blessing to our eyes who have so much poor printing to wade through), together with many curious and well-executed sketches of Africans in their various and ludicrous attitudes and proceedings. Regarding the map, we may be permitted to observe that the less that is said about it the better. Mr. Keith Johnston has doubtless executed it as he was instructed and commanded. The paper on which it is printed will, however, not stand much handling, a matter which is to be regretted. Speke might have brought something tougher from the Nile head, if he had found it out.

We now proceed forthwith to the book itself, and, *in limine*, we must observe that there were others connected with Speke's expedition—for his expedition he claims it to be. Foremost of the assistants on the original plan was that energetic individual, Consul Petherick. Captain Speke has incautiously and spitefully attacked him in the most ungenerous manner. This gentleman's case forms a most material portion of the whole subject, and Petherick's proceedings require to be cleared up and faithfully placed before the public. To do this will require more time and room than we could have wished to take. To avoid, however, every possibility of any charge of unfair suppression or misrepresentation of any portion of this part of the subject being made against us, we must have recourse to the full evidence of Captain Speke himself, and to the proceedings of the Royal Geographical Society in reference to the expedition placed by them under his charge. If in doing this we show a great failure of memory on the part of Speke in matters well known, or that could have readily been ascertained by him, we may justly be allowed to suspect the candour and plain dealing in other parts of his narratives and discoveries. Having done this fairly, we shall then allow Consul

Petherick and his heroic and devoted wife, who accompanied him up the Nile, to speak for themselves, through documents which have been placed at our disposal, and which, if we mistake not, will demand Captain Speke's serious attention.

We now beg the reader's special attention to the dates and narratives of the different parties concerned in the proceedings under review.

Captain Speke tells us (*Proceedings of the Royal Geographical Society*, vol. x., p. 89), March 24th, 1859, that "he had consequently proposed to Mr. Petherick to make a combined advance simultaneously with him on those tribes which are on the north of the Lake and due south of Gondokoro, and that Mr. Petherick had assented to co-operate with him; and as so much depended upon the security, or otherwise, of the undertaking, he hoped that that gentleman would receive the same support from the Government that he had done." Petherick, who was present, stated that, "although he was engaged in trade, and had five or six establishments to look after," yet, "he would not allow his friend to remain in the lurch while it was in his power to relieve him." It was May, 1859, that Speke's expedition was finally arranged. " Much about that time," says he, " Petherick, an ivory merchant, who had spent many years on the Nile, arrived in England and gratuitously offered, as it would not interfere with his trade, to place boats at Gondokoro, and send a party of men up the White Nile,"—" eventually to assist me on coming down." " Mr. Petherick showed a great zeal for geographical exploits; so, as I could not get money enough for all I intended to accomplish, I drew up a plan for him to ascend the Usua River " (supposed to be the chief tributary), " and did my best, through the medium of Earl de Grey and Ripon, then president of the Royal Geographical Society, to advance money to carry out these desirable objects."

Captain Speke shortly after this left England on his mission, but he had hardly done so when it was found out, as it ought at first to have been, that there were only two months in the year that vessels could move on the river, if river there was in that part of Africa, so it became necessary to make an arrangement for more safe and certain assistance.

The first plan proposed by Petherick (not by Speke) to the Royal Geographical Society, July

11th, 1859 (*Proceedings*, vol iv., pp. 223, 224,) which Speke alludes to and says (p. 608), "It would have been well for us both had he stuck to," was to place three well-armed boats at the base of the cataracts, beyond Gondokoro, by November, 1861, for the sum of 2000*l*. This sum the Government would not give. How, then, could Petherick have stuck to it? As an alternative, he then proposed for the sum of 1000*l*. "to place two well-provisioned and armed boats, under the superintendence of one of my own men, on whose integrity I could confidently depend, to await the arrival of the expedition at the above-named cataracts, from 1861, until June, 1862." This latter plan, of which Captain Speke was perfectly cognisant, was from necessity adopted by the parties concerned, and especially the Royal Geographical Society, June 11th, 1860, to aid the object (*Proceedings*, vol. iv., p. 222), "departed from their usual rules, and headed a subscription with 100*l*. towards defraying the expenses;" justly adding, that "Petherick could scarcely be expected to do it at his own expense." Indeed, he had previously told them (p. 225), "single-handed, I had not the means to achieve it." The 100*l*. that

Speke says he got Earl Ripon to advance Petherick was no doubt the 100*l.* subscription here mentioned as from the Royal Geographical Society.

It may here be advisable to bring forward the names of a few of the subscribers, &c., to the fund adverted to (*Proceedings*, vol. iv., p. 417), thus :—

Royal Geographical Society . .	£100
Foreign Office	100
William Speke	100
Consul Petherick	50

with many of the personal friends of the latter.

At the meeting of the Royal Geographical Society, November, 1861, it was announced that a subscription was decided on for the object, because the Government had declined to make any further grant (*Proceedings,* vol. v., p. 222). Speke knew this, but says not one word about it. The subscription was set on foot accordingly. The agreement between Petherick and the Society was made Feb. 6th and 8th, 1861 (*Proceedings*, vol. x., p. 60), and was, in substance, that Consul Petherick undertakes, " in consideration of the receipt of £1000 towards the expedition up the Nile, to place two well-armed boats during 1861 at Gondokoro, it being further understood that in the event of Captain Speke not having arrived at that time at Gondokoro, Consul Petherick shall not be bound to remain beyond June 1862." On the 8th July, 1861, the subscription had reached the sum of £1166 7s. (*Proceedings*, vol. v., p. 43), and the instructions for his guidance given to Petherick (July 8th, 1861), in a note, we find as follows:—" You will then, in the event of Captain Speke not having arrived before July, 1862, leave a trustworthy person, with sufficient provisions, in charge of the boats; the maintenance of these until June, 1862, being of primary importance." " The President and Council do not attempt to lay down any limit to this explanation," and adding " fully trusting to your known zeal and energy, feel assured that you will do all in your power to effect the above-mentioned object without serious loss to the party under your command. In entrusting you with the sum which has been subscribed for this purpose, the President and Council, considering themselves accountable to the subscribers for its proper expenditure, will require an account of all disbursements." Further, " the President and

Council take this opportunity of expressing their admiration at the spirit of enterprise which has induced you to undertake this enterprise; which has induced you, at great personal risk and considerable pecuniary loss, to undertake the charge of this expedition, and they hope, under God's providence, that you may not only succeed," &c.

Captain Speke's serious charges—serious, but unjust, charges—against Consul Petherick, made in the concluding pages of his book, began at and from his arrival at Gondokoro. He says, p. 603, " But what has become of Petherick? He was trading at Niambara, 70 miles due west of this, though he had, since I left him in England, raised a subscription of £1000 from those of my friends to whom this *Journal* is respectfully dedicated as the smallest return a grateful heart can give for their attempt to succour me on knowing the fate of the expedition was in great jeopardy. Arrived at Gondokoro, our first inquiry was, of course, for Petherick. A mysterious silence ensued. We were then informed that Debono was the man we had to thank for the assistance we had received in coming from Madi, and then in hot haste, after exchanging greetings with Mahomet's friend, who was Debono's agent here, we took leave of him to hunt up Petherick,"—but instead of him they found Mr. Baker.

This Debono, or as Mr. Baker in derision calls him, "that estimable British subject," was soon afterwards caught by Petherick carrying slaves down the river, and we believe sent by him in irons to Cairo, where he and his companions, making themselves to be Turks instead of Maltese, were, we believe, soon liberated by order of the British Government.

At this particular moment, says Speke, evidently in high spirits, " My men begged for some clothes, as Petherick, they said, had a store for me under the charge of his Vakil. The storekeeper was then called, and confirming the story of my men, I begged of him to give me what was my own. It turned out that the whole was Petherick's, but he had ordered to give me on account everything I wanted. This being settled, I took ninety-five yards of the commonest stuff as a makeshift for mosquito curtains for my men, besides four sailors' shirts for my head man. Almost immediately Petherick and his wife, accompanied by Dr. Murie, made their appearance, but with no welcome greetings like those given to the slave-traders' agent, when he (Petherick) told me he had brought a number of men carrying ivory, for the purpose now of seeking me on the east bank of the Nile by following its course to the south (what, carry ivory up to the head of the Nile?), though he had given up all hope of seeing me. He then offered me his *dyaber*, as well as anything else I wanted that lay within his power to give." The cold sarcastic reply was that Baker had supplied him with everything, and that "he had and to spare." " Yet, at his urgent request, I (Speke) took a few more yards of cloth for my men, and some cooking fat; and though I offered to pay, he declined to accept any return at my hands " (p. 607). He then also tells that " he separated from Grant at Kazeh (Jan., 1861), hurried from Uganda and his dear female friends there, solely to keep faith with him; " and amongst other things, said that he felt much annoyed at the disappointments Petherick had brought upon him; and, moreover, that everybody told him that Petherick could have gone to Faloro, and proceeded south from that place, had his trade on the west of the Nile not attracted him there (p. 603). Now, as Speke could not come down the Nile in boats, how was Petherick, with his boats, to go up it, over the various cataracts, and through districts without food ? Speke does not condescend to show this.

A few words are here necessary to show the error which the Royal Geographical Society committed in so hastily taking the mission out of Petherick's hands (*Proceedings*, vol. iv., p. 19). Mr. Galton, their present African guide, stated that the Nyambara, to which Petherick had gone, was the district where he had last been, or 300 miles further west. Mr. Baker rashly adopted the same opinion (*Proceedings*, vol. vii., p. 78, Khartoum, Nov. 24th, 1862). Had this been true, it would have been a great breach of faith ; but it was not so, but arose from the ignorance of what the name or word Niams, or Niam Niam, means. It is used by the trading and travelling Moslems to designate by way of reproach all the Southern Pagan population of Africa that are Pagans and asserted to be canibals, from the Nile to the sources of the Niger, and is used as a plea of justification for their invading, catching, and making them

slaves, it being held by Mahomedans as a sure passport to Paradise to catch a heathen and compel him
to be a slave or to adopt the tenets of Islamism.

Considering all these authentic details, it is
evident that Captain Speke's memory is very bad
and sadly at fault. We have dwelt upon them at
much length, because if we find such errors in
matters well known to him, or that could so readily
have been ascertained, it cannot fail to raise doubts
in the minds of observers about the author's accuracy
on other grave points, especially so in those where
his statements are clearly based upon foregone conclusions. In our opinion, not much reliance can be
placed on statements made by such biassed authority.
The questions also under consideration are public
property; the parties engaged in them are public
servants, and it is therefore absolutely necessary to
know who should be believed when anything is
wrong, or appears to be wrong. We have it now
under Captain Speke's own hand, that he did obtain
supplies at Gondokoro, sent there by Petherick's
forethought, about one year before he reached that
place; and we shall presently, from incontrovertible
evidence, learn that Petherick had furnished further

most abundant supplies, placed ready at the same place before Speke reached it, and that this was known to him when he made the culpable accusations that he has done.

Let us attend to dates. The last-mentioned transaction with Petherick took place at Gondokoro, on the 18th February, just three days after Speke and Grant had reached that place.

Captain Speke left England on his last mission, April, 1860. He reached and started from the African coast, opposite Zanzibar, on October 1st of the same year. Two or three months later we find him at Kazeh, with all his supplies exhausted. On the same authority (President's Address, May 27th, 1861), we find him near Kazeh on September 30th, 1861, with his supplies replenished. On the 7th February, 1862, he reached Uganda, and on the 15th February, 1863, he reached Gondokoro, having in two years and a half travelled by land in direct lines about 1300 geographical miles; but eighteen months after himself and the wiseheads in London had fixed that he could be, and should be.

Consul Petherick, on the other hand, left England on his auxiliary mission in May or June, 1861, and after a detention of six weeks at Korsoko, on the great bend of the Nile, for want of camels and by sickness, he reached Khartoum, from whence, on the 18th of November, 1861, he despatched two boats with expert explorers and supplies for Speke, both of which boats reached Gondokoro in regular time. He himself proceeded with four other hired boats, such as he could pick out, for the same destination. On the 30th of March he reached the country of the Shilluks, and on the 7th of April the mouth of the Sobat, in about 9° 11′ N. lat., and not, as Speke says (p. 603), in lat. 7° N., where he was encountered by the foul south winds, which checked his progress, and which was attended with all those disastrous delays and fatal consequences which are already partly known, but presently to be more particularly alluded to. As one instance of the delay thus occasioned, he took seven days to reach Lake No, or Nuvier, from the Sobat, which in a former voyage, and at the proper season, he had performed in one day.

Consul Petherick, finding it was impossible for him to proceed at that time by the river, left it and proceeded by land to Mouson, the capital of Nyambara,

a former commercial depôt of his. His journey by
land was almost as difficult and dangerous as that by
the river, occupying about two months in a distance
of about 70 miles. There he abode till the beginning
of February, 1863, on account of the season, but
more on account of bad health amongst his party.
He sent his old boats back to Khartoum, with particular instructions to send up immediately three
more well armed and manned, with abundance of
supplies for Speke and his party, according as such
might be required. To meet this large outlay he
collected, at much inconvenience, all his ready
available property, amounting from 3000l. to 4000l.
These three fresh boats and their supplies, we learn
from Mr. Baker, Khartoum, Nov. 8, 1862 (*Proceedings*, vol. vii., p. 49), were then nearly ready to
depart, and would leave Khartoum with his force on
the 12th of December. They all left December
13th, the united force consisting of six boats and
200 armed men. They reached Gondokoro on the
1st of February, two weeks before Speke reached
that place. Petherick expressly tells that when he
reached Gondokoro on the 18th of February, he
found, besides what his two early boats brought up,

another boat that left Khartoum with himself and the three last alluded to, and that left with Baker.

The letter from Petherick above alluded to was transmitted by Petherick's brother-in-law to Sir Roderick Murchison, the worthy and respected President of the Royal Geographical Society. At his particular request the portion we are about to quote was struck out, he, with his characteristic good feeling, wishing to preserve peace amongst those explorers, and probably also, at the time, considering it impossible that Captain Speke could have acted as he has done. Speke's unguarded publication must, if we mistake not, give Sir Roderick both annoyance and pain; but it may also teach him that all men are not so straightforward and honest as himself. The part of the letter struck out commences after the words in the *Athenæum*, " effected according to their own account with trifling difficulties to themselves " thus:—

" It is with much regret I have to notice Speke's coolness and ill-treatment of us. He would or could not understand the difficulties and sacrifices we had put ourselves to, to meet him; and having helped himself from our stores to sundry blue cloth and other indispensable necessaries for the clothing of his men prior to our arrival, he heaped insult to injury upon us by refusing our boats and provisions, preferring those of Mr. Samuel Baker, then present, notwithstanding our representation that the whole had been paid for, and were expected to supply him with every necessary.

" Grant was throughout *the gentleman*, but Speke I shall never forgive. Our engagement to meet him, he said, had virtually expired in July, 1862, and he now would purchase any article he required. How indignantly this was refused you may imagine; but the crowning piece of all his ill-temper was the ignoring of my expedition, ending with the inquiry as to whom he had proposed it! He was, however, rather astonished at my repartee, that my meeting him was proposed by himself, and his letter to that effect was still, doubtless, preserved by the Council of the Geographical Society. His jealousy was so aggravated as to lead him to declare he required no succour dodge! Although he had had ample experience of the violences, robbery, and slave kid-napping propensities of the traders to the aborigines, he was dumb upon the subject; but when I stated that—travelling through districts long ruined by them, and where the natives would not employ themselves as porters for anything short of a cow or bullock each, and that far in the interior we could neither return nor advance without them— our men had joined a party of traders in a razzia to supply us with the needful cattle, and restore some sixty head already borrowed from a trader for former negro services, Speke would make no allowance for our peculiar circumstances or the alacrity of our men (although much against our will) to pay the negroes out for former wanton assaults against ourselves; and I will not be surprised that Speke and Baker, hand in glove, will make some ill-natured remark on the subject at home. However, as nothing that has transpired will be withheld from the public, with a clear conscience I will willingly abide their decision."

In a subsequent letter he says :—

"To add insult to injury flesh and blood cannot bear it; and while not wishing to depreciate the labours of others, I am determined to maintain my own."

In a very plain letter, from Consul Petherick,

dated Bahr el Ghazal, May 12, 1863, and which appears, though not at full length, in a contemporary of great circulation and high authority (*The Athenæum* of Aug. 29, 1863), we have a full account of the dangers and difficulties that Petherick had to encounter in his endeavour to reach Gondokoro, and during which voyage, as Mr. Baker admits, they had lost nearly all their valuable supplies by damage and shipwreck.   But distressing as this narrative is, it is still far below the sad evils which the journal of his heroic wife, placed in our hands for perusal, has given of the voyage.   Cold, callous, and unfeeling must the head and the heart of any reasonable being be, who can peruse either without the bitterest sorrow.   Of the chief facts contained therein Captain Speke must have been well acquainted, as Dr. Murie, who was one of the sufferers, no doubt told him at Gondokoro.   It is therefore almost incredible that, in the face of such facts, and in possession of the knowledge of all matters connected with these events as we have shown him to have been, and the statements in his own pages, he could have brought the cruel and unfounded charges against Consul Petherick that he has done, and imply, as it would appear, that all the difficulties and wilful delays which he had encountered were owing to the misconduct of Petherick alone.

Independent of the testimony of Petherick we have the certain testimony of Speke and Baker that abundant supplies and aid had reached Gondokoro before Speke did, but of this and the voyage of Petherick's three boats which accompanied Baker, neither he nor Speke take the slightest notice. This is most reprehensible. Those supplies, consisting of many things, such as beer, wine, rice, soup, pearl barley, Le Mann's biscuits, a gutta percha boat, &c., were sold to the Dutch ladies, who were not a little rejoiced to find such luxuries there, and they enjoyed them famously (*Proceedings*, vol. vii., p. 14, Nov. 23rd, 1863). Moreover, Colonel Rigby, late Consul at Zanzibar, told the Royal Geographical Society, Nov. 24, 1862, and he is a very competent judge, that it was fortunate that Petherick did not get to Gondokoro sooner, as, if he had, it would have been injurious to Speke's progress. He also told them at the same time about the dreadful famine that raged over all Eastern Tropical Africa at the time Speke and Grant entered it, so that ten able-bodied slaves were purchased for one bullock.

Consul Petherick has, therefore, in every way, clearly fulfilled his agreement with the Royal Geographical Society, and it is with them only that he has to do as regards the subscription fund. He has done more than he even agreed to do. He received the sum of £1000 out of that fund. Mrs. Petherick's journal confirms this, and Dr. Murie, who made out the account, can tell, if he has not already told, the subscribers to the fund that a larger sum was actually expended at the very outset at Khartoum. The balance, therefore, whatever that may be, belongs to Petherick until his expenses are liquidated down to the time that the expedition was unguardedly, and, as we think, ungenerously taken from his hands and given to Mr. Baker, whose appearance on the scene so suddenly is somewhat remarkable. Moreover, as the Society did not limit the extent and time of this auxiliary force, it is, we presume, legally liable for the additional expenditure that Petherick has incurred. Instead of Speke calling upon Petherick to account for his intermission, he must call upon Baker for his, when we shall see what Speke's further expenses have been, and what Baker has been paid, and which, whatever they were, he has bound himself to pay, if exceeding the sum of £2800—£2500 from the British Government, and £300 from the Government of the Cape of Good Hope.

It was not Petherick who gratuitously offered himself for this expedition, but Speke, as we have seen, who proposed it to him and the Society. This fund also was not collected, as Speke says it was, for extricating him and his expedition from failure, when his friends in England became informed of the difficulties that he had encountered. Petherick put £1000 of it in his pocket, and at Khartoum, months before, Speke's friends heard of his difficulties; and when they did hear of this it was with the account that it required only to have his supplies replenished to enable him to go on. Moreover, the fund was obtained, not for the purpose of aiding him in his southern travels, but to afford him assistance in his descent of the Upper Nile after he had reached that part of his journey, and to aid him in going down the Nile from Gondokoro to Egypt.

Captain Speke's difficulties, great as they were,

and we do not wish to underrate them, might in our opinion have been greatly lessened, if not altogether prevented, by common prudence and proper caution, good temper and patience. So also ought the proper funds to have been obtained in this country by those who planned and got up this expedition. Gentlemen in England seem to have no idea of the expenses of even ordinary travelling in this portion of Africa. The Dutch ladies, so repeatedly heard of, are spending at the rate of £6000 per annum; and Speke tells us that the urgency of his demand for porters and supplies obliged him to offer " three times " the wages that the merchants were wont to give, or could afford to give. Speke, as Captain Grant informs us, replenished his stores and supplies from Arab traders in the interior at the rate of 1600 per cent. In other places the natives demand a bullock now instead of a few beads as formerly for the same labour. Thus the money goes, and all this shows that the people, rude as they are, yet retain some glimmerings of common sense, and so far as to know that as labour and property come more and more into demand they ought to obtain more for both.

We are far from wishing to cast blame on any party for the delays and difficulties that have taken place in this African expedition; but at the same time it is right to show that the person most liable to censure is Captain Speke, who was much more beyond his set time in coming to a given point. Here Consul Petherick was not to blame. The greatest error of the latter was that he attempted at too late a period in the season to push on to Gondokoro, just as Speke selected a most improper season for his expedition, and the route that he took to carry out his object. The Sultan of Zanzibar told him his proper road was from Mombas, where 300 miles, instead of 1100 miles, would bring him in sight of the Nile head, and through a country by no means difficult or barren. This error was Speke's, and the road was of his selection, and we hope that what has taken place will tend to prevent the Royal Geographical Society from committing such another blunder in future.

The sufferings of Consul Petherick and his wife, who accompanied him in this unhappy journey, have indeed been severe. On the report of their death, eagerly circulated in Egypt and in Europe by their bitter enemies the African slave-traders, who told lies to injure him, Petherick's credit was completely stopped. All letters from their European friends and correspondents were detained, and left unheeded in the office of the British Consul-General for Egypt at Cairo, so that for many months, and even down to the latest period, they were left wholly ignorant of what was passing in England against them; while, be it remarked, every communication addressed to Mr. Baker was carefully forwarded. An established business, the labour of many years, has been nearly if not wholly ruined, the health of himself and his talented wife, it may be said, totally destroyed, so that to attend to any business is out of the husband's power; while at the same time his office as Consul in that part of Africa runs the greatest risk of being cut off; as it may appear to our Government that in such a country the duties of a British Consul and the business of a merchant are incompatible with each other. At Khartoum it was publicly stated that his life would be taken by assassination on the part of the vindictive slave-traders. The Royal Geographical Society, and also the Foreign Office, acted very wrong to press and to encourage Petherick to take the charge of such an expedition; while he himself acted equally wrong and unguarded by accepting such a charge for such a low sum, and without a specific guarantee from both that all proper expenses incurred should be made good to him whatever the result of the work was. Fine promises, plaudits, and praises made in the Royal Geographical Society's meetings will not butter parsnips, nor avert the poverty from the Consul and his family which may be the result of this ill-starred expedition. These ill-used individuals most unquestionably deserve, and ought to obtain, something more than pity and commiseration from the quarters mentioned, instead of the reproaches and insults launched against them from any one or from any quarter recognised by these parties; while no compensation that either can give can compensate the losses and anguish that the Consul and his wife have suffered.

Before concluding this portion of our subject, and entering upon the geographical, commercial, and political portions of the work before us, we would forcibly observe, and draw the attention of all parties interested in the matter to the fact, that the passport for the passage of Speke and Grant through the remote and unstable and grasping interior of that division of Africa was in the promises lavishly made by Speke of the great presents and wealth that the chiefs would receive as soon as he met Petherick, his servant and subordinate, to obtain all the fine things that he was bringing forward for him to give to them. We cannot find that one step has been taken by Speke to redeem his promises of payment to those chiefs for aid given and for courtesies shown by these great men. On the contrary, we find Mr. Baker, the deputy for them, instead of going south and south-west as we were told he meant to do in order to gain the shores of Nyanza, has gone to the south-east and east from Gondokoro, in quite a different direction. This change and forgetfulness of promises brings to our remembrance the adage, " out of sight out of mind ; " but which neglect and omission may result in unfavourable consequences to any future traveller from England or British India, who may think of completing what Speke has certainly left undone.

No. II.—MANNERS AND CUSTOMS.

BEFORE entering upon the geographical, political, and commercial portion of the volume, it appears advisable to advert to the subject of the life, manners, and customs of some of the tribes of these interior portions of Africa, who are represented to us as more polished than ourselves, and as equal to our gay neighbours on the other side of the Channel. We shall in this be as short as possible, and, as far as decency will admit it, make the narrative clear. Two States, Karagwe and Uganda, may be deemed sufficient for the purpose mentioned. Speke seems to have a peculiar delight in dwelling upon such subjects, and also as showing off his great knowledge and research in antique lore in his new and remarkable theories and references.

We take Karagwe first. This is a very hilly country, the hills extending to the shores of the lake, or supposed lake. The chief or king, Rumanika, is a frank outspoken fellow, and has evidently more in him than Speke himself is willing to allow.

His people and himself have no knowledge of God or of a human soul; man and the bullock in this respect standing on an equal footing. Marriage is a mere question of money. A man accused is immediately torn to pieces; if the accused endeavour to plead his defence, his voice is at once drowned, and the miserable victim dragged off in the roughest manner to death. Rumanika warned Speke that as he went forward " he must not expect to find again a reasonable man like myself," and soon after increases the compliment by eulogising Speke (p. 241) thus, " without doubt he had never seen such a wise man as myself." This amiable and polished king, in respect for his father's (Dagara) memory, instead of putting his body " under ground, the people erected a hut over him, and thrusting in five maidens and fifty cows, enclosed the doorway in such a manner that the whole of them subsequently died of pure starvation" (p. 221). Rumanika has five wives, milk drinkers, and fatted up like the following lady, the wife of his brother. We must give this precious piece of information in Speke's words, as he seems to delight and excel in such exhibitions. An agreement was quickly made with the lady. Speke was to obtain a good view of her naked, and then to measure her, upon a like reciprocity on his part. After getting her "to sidle and wriggle into the midst of the hut, I did as I promised." With bare limbs and shirt sleeves well tucked up, Speke began his measuring and, as he called it, " engineering" process, thus :—Round the arm, 1 ft. 11 in. ; chest, 4 ft. 4 in.; thickest part of the thigh, 2 ft. 7 in. ; calf, 1 ft. 8 in.; height, 5 ft. 8 in. The height, we are told, is not quite certain, because he could not get her laid upon the floor ; " yet, after infinite exertions on the part of us both, this was accomplished, when she sank down again," &c. " Beside her sat her daughter, a lass of sixteen, stark naked, sucking at a milk-pot, on which her father kept her at work by holding a rod in his hands." " I got up a bit of a flirtation with Missy, and induced her to rise and shake hands with me. Her features were lovely, but her body was as round as a ball."

We believe none of our readers ever met with or ever heard of such a piece of " engineering" as this, and we dare say will never wish to meet with such another.

Captain Speke, in a long and learned disquisition, tries to prove from the Bible that Zerah, the Ethiopian, was one of the chief progenitors of the Wahuma, in Karagwe and Uganda; and that the Rumanika and his family, and also the Waganda, were the lineal descendants of the great Jewish King David, " whose hair," Captain Speke assures this black African monarch, " was as straight as his (Speke's) own." That they all were one family with the Abyssinians, with whose king, Sahela Selasseh, Queen Victoria had exchanged presents. Now, Sahela Selasseh was merely, and yesterday only, the king of Shoa, a revolted province of Abyssinia, and not the great empire of Abyssinia itself, especially as it stood in very ancient times. Moreover, King David, we are told from the best authority, " was ruddy, and withal of a beautiful countenance (fair of eyes), and goodly to look upon." (1st Sam. c. xvi., v. 12.) So that David's progeny are sadly degenerated to have become wholly black. Nor do we think that Speke will gain anything by his announcement that his hair is like King David's. Further, if Zerah, the Ethiopian (A.C. 941), had

Uganda and Karagwe as part of his dominions, it will follow that Zerah must have been well acquainted with the source and tributaries of the Nile; and though the records of his empire are lost to us, still his knowledge of all these things was long before Speke so pompously proclaimed the discovery. It would be a waste of time to attempt to investigate such crude speculations further. They do not, however correct they may be, prove that Captain Speke has discovered the Source or Spring of the Nile.

King Rumanika appears after all to be a bit of a wag. At p. 236 he asks Speke, " Whether or not the moon made different faces to laugh at us mortals on earth." Of this there can be little doubt, and well and properly may the moon do so. Let any one look at the moon when she is full, and then say if she does not represent a photograph of Speke, back uppermost, with both legs stretched out, and arms extended, grasping the mountains of the Moon, the Lake Nyanza, the hills of Chope (the Apennines of the Moon), and Luta Nzigé, the Man portion of the satellite, and other points similar in both. In short, the keen-eyed Rumanika appears to have been laughing at Speke's credulity.

From Karagwe we proceed to Uganda, peopled by a branch of the Zerah family, the best blood of Abyssinia. This is a kingdom that we are told all ought to imitate and to admire—where the population are described as dwelling in a perfect paradise, and all most respectably dressed. On looking into the matter fully, however, we perceive that this splendid dress consists of bark cloth and the hides of cows and wild beasts, &c., where such can be obtained. The population are subject to a most bloody and brutal tyrant. Culprits are dismembered bit by bit, as food for the vultures, till life is extinct. The King shoots whomsoever he pleases, at times, and in mere sport. His brothers, however many there may be, are all burnt to death at his coronation, with the exception of two or three to preserve the succession in case the King is cut off without children. He keeps a harem of upwards of 300 females, furnished frequently by their parents, in order to defray the confiscation that the sovereign of his own jealousy or pleasure is daily heaping upon them. This King, we are informed " keeps a splendid court," yet we are told that he sometimes ate with a copper knife and picker, not forked, but more usually like a dog with both hands (p. 392). Every day saw one, two, or three poor females dragged from the harem to a cruel execution and death. In one day and at one time no fewer than four were thus dragged forth. At page 357, in proof of their modesty and decency, Speke informs us minutely thus:—" These twenty naked virgins, the daughters of Wakungu, all smeared and streaming with grease, each holding a small square of Mbugu for a fig leaf, marched in a line before us as a fresh addition to the harem." After this presentation, " a sedate old dame rose from the squatting mass, ordered the virgins to right about, and marched them off, showing their still more naked reverse."

When the people wish to penetrate into futurity, they sacrifice a child, and of so little value is human life in Uganda, that when the King heard that the white man intended to visit him, he sacrificed 50 big men and 400 small ones. In short, every part of the State appears to be one vast scene of plunder, robbery, violence, slavery, the slave trade, and bloodshed, accompanied by frequent famines and want. Speke himself often went, at least so he says, supperless to bed, and without food for the day; his men eating grass.

We have noticed the refined manners of the higher class of males. Let us turn to that of the females—the Queen Dowager, for example. She appears to be the best of the lot, and has some fun about her. Speke was a particular favourite with her—so much so that her courtiers said he had bewitched her heart. Her Majesty held a particular levee and party for his reception. She appeared in great state, and had at hand plenty of the best Pombe in the kingdom. A large wooden trough was placed before the Queen and filled with liquor. The Queen and her ministers plunged into the Pombe and became uproarious. The Queen put her head to the trough and drank like a pig from it, and was followed by her ministers. Speke, the friend and invited guest, ought in courtesy or good manners to have done the same. Flattery was applied to the lady, who was led to believe that as often as she changed her dress she improved in beauty. She changed dresses three times, and

each time swilled Pombe largely.* The Queen and
her councillors all became uproarious. She began
to sing, and the councillors to join in the chorus;
then all sang, and all drank and drank and sang,
till in their native excitement they turned the
palace into a pandemonium. Now, all of a sudden,
as if the Devil had taken possession of the company,
the ministers, with all the courtiers, jumped to their
legs—cups were too small, so the trough was
resorted to, and the Queen graced it by drinking,
pig-fashion, first, and then handing it round to the
company.

This model State and splendid capital (so Speke
writes Petherick) was his great object, and it may
be presumed congenial to his feelings and pursuits.
He boldly insisted that as " he was a great Prince
in his own country," so it would be a degradation
to him to reside in the customary places allotted

* At a particular stage of this debauch, says Speke (p. 314), an
eye-witness to the act, " a naked virgin, with a Mbugu only,
handed to the Queen over her shoulder a cup of pombe," Speke
looking on. Mbugu is a favourite word with our author. It
occurs in almost every page. It is made of bark-cloth, of a shape
as female fancy dictates. As far as we can gather the meaning of
the name, it signifies not to cover, but to show the part that
should be covered.

to travellers, and that in the palace was his proper home, where he could conveniently see and converse with the King every day without the presence or the intervention of his ministers. He stuck to this point, and by the aid and influence of the Queen Dowager he gained it. Now, what would the people of England say if King Mtésa should send one of his princes, or ministers, as ambassador to the British sovereign, and wish that this minister—a " first-rate noble, the hangman or cook "—should reside in Buckingham Palace or Windsor Castle, and be at liberty to communicate with Queen Victoria daily, without the intervention of her ministers; and further, that she should maintain Mtésa's ambassador and suite at her sole expense? Yet even more than this is what Speke demands, for he had no diplomatic character. Why, such a demand would be considered a national insult, and the insulters at once ordered about their business, and to leave the country. Mtésa ought to have served Speke in this manner.

We are almost moved to tears at the pathetic complaints and woes of Speke, who, though living in a splendid and well-peopled palace, yet found

himself so lonely, without a wife or female companion, that very frequently he could neither sleep
nor eat. This deprivation of domestic comfort seems
to have worked like " a Bee i' the bonnet." When
at the Ripon Falls, he states (p. 470)—" This day
I sat watching the fish playing at the falls, and felt
as if I only wanted a wife and family, garden and
yacht, rifle and rod, to make me happy here for life,
so charming was the place. What a place, I
thought to myself, this would be for missionaries.
They never could fear starvation," &c. Now, as
to all this loneliness and want of female society, we
find (p. 309) that the Commander-in-Chief of the
army had, by the hand of an elderly Mganda woman,
sent him a lady, with metaphorical compliments,
praying that " I would accept her to carry my
water," and adding that if I did not like her, or
wanted one that might be thought prettier, I could
have a choice of one amongst ten of all colours.
" As nothing offends so much as rejecting such
presents, I kept her for the time being." The
Queen Dowager afterwards made him a present of
two, declaring he might have more, and consequently we find she had sent him another, which

Speke intimated he did not think good enough for a man of his dignity. She replied that the one sent was only "a creature" such as they bestowed upon personages of inferior rank; therefore if he wanted something better, he must wait a bit. The King in the meantime had (p. 284) sent him one. Speke therefore was not and could not be in great want of African wives or maidens to carry his water. And as regards a real wife, his friend Rumanika would have readily given him the pick of his kingdom; and surely Captain Speke could have felt no degradation in marrying a lineal descendant of the great Jewish King David. She would have been a curiosity in this country, and a credit and triumph to him amongst his true friends in England.

There are two great omissions amongst the views given in the volume. First, Speke's " engineering" on the Fat Queen, and secondly, the Queen Dowager of Uganda and her courtiers drinking Pombe in pig-fashion, and Speke "n'yanzigging" or looking on, applauding the scene. Two drawings of those acts upon a tolerably large scale, finished and hung up, one in the Foreign Office and one in the library, or some room of the Royal Geographical Society, would form objects of attraction such as have not been seen in the latter office since Du Chaillu's gorilla graced the room. Both views would draw a large number of gazers and amuse the Council in the one place, and in the other inspire the secretary, tickle the clerks, and amuse foreign ambassadors while waiting for the appointed interview.

But here we must conclude our observations, perhaps too far extended, upon such miserable subjects and senseless narratives, but with which more than two hundred pages of the volume is filled. It is with a disgust that we want proper words to express, to find the first names in Europe prostituted, and especially the name of our great and gracious Sovereign insulted and degraded, in giving names to places in this most barbarous and degraded country. We earnestly hope that the Royal Geographical Society will in future denounce with the greatest severity all such proceedings on the part of any one they patronise and employ.

Nothing can be so absurd as to impose English names on any part, but especially upon places in the remote interior parts of Africa. This is, we believe, done by no other nation. What nonsense it is calling a part of Lake Nyanza the Bengal Archipelago. A stagnant puddle, with water in it only during the rains, or when the lake overflows, the Jordans, a name never heard of in geography. The eminent characters seized upon to give names to Ripon Falls, Murchison Creek—a stagnant puddle—can scarcely feel gratified by this appropriation of their names. It is really time that such tomfoolery should be relinquished. To what do we owe so much of our ignorance of ancient geography but to the substitution by later travellers of new for ancient native names?—which are generally most expressive, whereas the names now so frequently given explain nothing. When such a promontory as the Cape of Good Hope, never before seen or known to geography in any age of the world, was discovered, it was reasonable and proper to give it the name it has obtained; and so of other places made known under similar circumstances. The Royal Geographical Society of London should attend to this subject, as the world should look up to it as the leader and director in all such matters.

It is truly deplorable to learn that all intercourse with white men only extends the slave trade and slavery and desolation over Africa, and especially in the large districts at present under our notice. Speke says they have brought " the devil " into that portion of Africa. Baker tells us that they have rendered Gondokoro " a perfect hell." The whole river is now frequented by Turks, Circassians, Syrians, and, according to Dr. Murie, the worst description of Italians and Frenchmen. The following letter, received from sure authority, and dated " Khartoum, Nov. 12, 1863," will show in a strong light what is now going on there :—

' You have no idea how dreadful the slave trade is here. The longer we stay the more we find it out. Last Sunday I saw three boats full of slaves shipped off to Cairo or Kordofan by the Government, guarded by soldiers. Oh, it was such a shocking sight! The Government pretend they do not allow slavery, but they accept slaves in payment from the people here for their taxes. It is a burning shame; I cannot write all the horrors of it. It makes one quite giddy. They look so pitiful, with great collars round their necks, and some with chains on their legs. Too much cannot be said against it.'

In its proper place we have forgotten to notice the important fact that Speke seems well acquainted with the proceedings of Petherick's first two explorers, for he tells us that they had proceeded a long way due south from Nyambara, and at this utmost point " found a river running from east to west." Petherick tells us that they went seventeen days' journey due south, when they were forced to turn back on account of famine and the hostility of the natives. At 10 geographical miles each day this distance would bring them to 2° 15′ N. lat., but nine miles per day to 1° 28′ N. lat., the latter to the Karuma Falls, and the former near to Kamrasi's palace. At the Karuma Falls the river runs from east to west; but we have yet to receive an account of this from Petherick himself, as also his latitudes and longitudes, which Dr. Murie tells us were taken at different places. But as regards this southern journey the account may be defective, because Mussard, his most faithful and trustworthy servant, was killed by an Arab soon after he joined his master, coming up the river. Mussard had left

Gondokoro about the end of June, 1862, at which time Speke had not reached that place. We are, however, indebted to Speke for noticing the subject, as it shows that those men had not been idle, and they had carried out their instructions as far as they could. In like manner we may allude to Speke's dictatorial letter of March, 1862 (*Proceedings*, vol. vii., p. 235), to Petherick, from the capital of Uganda, commanding him, as his superior officer, to come without delay to that place, with a great load of fine things to give to the kings of the country, adding that he (Speke) was well aware that he (Petherick) could not do this without a serious loss to his private affairs, but also telling him not to mind that, as whatever that loss might be, he would " ask the Government to defray it! " This declaration shows clearly that Petherick was not bound or expected to leave entirely his mercantile pursuits for the sole purpose of watching and looking for and guarding Speke and his expedition.

No. III.—GEOGRAPHY, COMMERCE, &c.

THE expedition of Burton and Speke, and next of Speke and Grant, so lately concluded, were both, but especially the latter, organised upon erroneous and fallacious principles. They went into Africa with a high hand, proclaiming loudly their great dignity and power, and the power and the greatness of their country. There were with them large parties of armed men, with numerous attendants, and extensive supplies. The chiefs and people were everywhere alarmed, knowing, as every one in Eastern Africa knows, what British power has effected in India. The most exaggerated reports were circulated about them, founded, as there is too much reason to believe, upon the foolish boastings made by individuals amongst the explorers. The miserable districts they had to pass through were quickly stripped of their scanty supplies. Enormous prices were demanded for all supplies of food and labour. The more rapidly the explorers hurried on, the more the chiefs and people exacted. They were attacked, plundered, deceived, laughed at, or dreaded, according as circumstances and opportunity offered. Wherever they came every person considered them fair game; that they would either never see them again, or if again, see them only as rulers or oppressors. The stories circulated to their prejudice flew about widely. A story also, however absurd, never loses in telling by Africans or Arabs, and the incautious boastings of the preceding Spekeite explorers ran before the second expedition, and gave rise to some delusive and ludicrous fears and opinions. The people in the interior were taught to believe that the travellers were cannibals; that being Anglo-Indians they would consume all their corn and their plantains, drink the Nyanza Lake dry, and blow up Africa!

Captain Speke, at all times, did everything to proclaim his contempt for trade, but which is the only passport in Africa. It is amusing to learn the cunning with which the chiefs and their retainers baffled all his wisdom and calculations in the collection of their customs and revenue. Suwarora, Vikory, and Kamrasi were all adepts in that way, and beat European tax-gatherers hollow. We hope

Speke will bring none of them here to collect our miscellaneous and income taxes,

Leaving for a time the consideration of Captain Speke's decisions about the different races of mankind, we proceed to analyse his geography. This important point connected with this portion of Africa, as adverted to in very ancient and later times, we must, however, condense as much as possible, but the narratives of eminent authors during a period of more than 3000 years cannot be placed in a column of our paper. Captain Speke would leave little to be said except what he himself has discovered or supposes he has discovered To complete his present geographical intelligence, we must return for a moment to the account of his former journey, as we find it in *Blackwood's Magazine*, October, 1859, and in the *Journal of the Royal Geographical Society*, vol. xxix., for 1859.

In his first journey Speke found Muanza, on the southern shore of a lake, or say of the lake, to be in 2° 31′ S. lat., and by " dead reckoning " due N. of Kazeh, that place being in 33° 1′ 34″ E. long. ; but we have good grounds to believe that Muanza is about 20′ further west, or in 32° 41′ E. long.

Satsuma, or Observatory Hill, was 15 miles to the eastward, and in 2° 24′ S. lat. From Muanza to Kitangule Karagwe is one month's journey by land, but only five days' voyage N.N.W. by water, which will bring the point on Karagwe to 1° 43′ S. lat., and 31° 35′ E. long. The Nyanza inundates extensively the land on its south side, because it is flush with the level surface of the country. Muanza stands on the east side of what is ludicrously called the Jordans, a creek or inlet of the lake extending a short distance south-east, like a bullock's curved horn. Eastward of Muanza 15 miles is Satsuma, or Observatory Hill, 2° 24′ S. lat., and northward of it, 15 miles in the lake, is the island of Ukerewe, from which the Arabs give the lake or sea its name. East of Satsuma 35 geographical miles Speke saw a small hill at the south-east corner of the lake. From thence the lake trended north, by Urudi or Uroro, opposite to islands Mazita and Ukerewe. Beyond this to the north, say 70 or 80 miles, lay the island of Thiri or Kitiri, which we find is to the south-east, and on the border of Uganda. Westward of Muanza the lake extended about the same distance as on the east side, making its breadth from east to west 80 geographical miles ; but stretching away to the northward like a long Lancaster gun to 3° 30′ N. lat. To the W.S.W. of Muanza the lake was studded with small islands, rising from 200 to 300 feet high, as far as the eye could reach ; the country of the Masai at a distance stretching eastward in little rolling hills.

This is what Speke saw with his eyes and heard with his ears in 1857, and which was exhibited as a wonderful object. By-and-by, however, the extensive noddle of this lake was cut off; then another and another portion, till it was brought into its present shape, and its northern edge close to the Equator. In the meantime, and at the same time, slice after slice was severed from its right cheek, and its first shape totally obliterated. Let the reader now attend to us. From about thirty miles east of the meridian of Muanza to Kagera, and not very much to the south of the same parallel as the head of the Jordans, Speke gives the land between Nyanza and Lake Tanganyika, 300 feet lower than Lake Nyanza. Next come for our consideration "the Mountains of the Moon." These were first laid down in a neat little circle as hills north of the

Tanganyika, but they are now removed about 1° 30′ further west, and to within a few miles of the Equator, and placed in a most conspicuous circle, in form like a Lord Chancellor's wig. The history of these Moon Mountains of Speke, for he is their parent, as also the christener of them as they stand, is somewhat curious. They were first given to be 6,000 feet above the level of the sea, but in a few months they grew up in Whitehall-place to 8,000 feet; and now the new ones have grown up prodigiously, as we shall presently see, while the Urundi batch have sunk to about 5,000 feet. Burton told an acquaintance of ours that the height of those hills at the head of Lake Tanganyika was only 2,000 feet above the level of the lake, instead of 8,000 feet!

We now come to the consideration of the last journey of Speke, for no one else can be taken into the narrative. We have seen that the lake floods the land on its southern shores extensively, and the same authority (Speke) tells us repeatedly that the lake on the north side never inundates its shore. When returned from his last journey he gave the height of the lake 3,550 feet—(see map published by Stanford, Charing-cross, by his permission and direction)—now he has raised it, on what we may call his official map, to its former height, 3,745 feet. Let us take it so, and notice the indescribable confusion and impossible results that must follow. Little Lake Windermere, 3,639 feet high, feeds, we are told, the Kitangule river, and this river runs into the Lake Nyanza, 3,745 feet high, thus making the river run upwards instead of downwards! No wonder the natives were afraid lest Speke's army should drink Nyanza dry, when we find that one draught sucked up 200 feet of its depth, in a surface of 9,000 square miles, particularly as he told us that South Nyanza was not very deep. Another suck, nay, even less, would have emptied it.*

Still more serious errors and inconsistencies than the one that has just been adverted to appear as we advance to the eastward. Mtésa's palace stands on a small eminence, and immediately adjoining it on

---

* This great decrease of the lake may have taken place in the year 1861, when Egypt was so nearly drowned. The decrease in the lake is now, as regards space, in both cases about equal to the increase in the other. It is therefore strange that Speke does not think of this in order to make out his second statement. This would have been plausible.

the west side is the end of Murchison Creek, a still inlet without current. This palace, or capital, is 3,400 feet above the level of the sea, but then it is still 345 feet below what is supposed to be the lake. There ought, therefore, to have been a strong rush and current of water northward in this creek, but there was none!

Again, at the Ripon Falls, only a few miles from the entrance to the Napoleon Channel, the elevation of the river above the level of the sea is stated to be 3,308 feet, and consequently it is there 339 feet below the lake. There must then have been a very great cataract, indeed, at the separation of the stream from the Nyanza. Yet the current as seen was very gentle. Again, the Ripon Falls had only 12 feet descent, yet we find at Urondogani, 0° 52′ 27″ north latitude, about 16 miles north, the river, in the intervening space gentle, stated to be 2,865 feet above the ocean, giving a descent to that place, of 883 feet in a distance of probably only 30 miles. At the Karuma Falls the river is stated to be 2,970 feet above the ocean, which is 105 feet above Urondogani, thus making the river for the space of 90 miles to run upwards instead of downwards.

Again, at Namaouji, 14 miles north of the capital of Uganda, we find the elevation of the land 3,103 feet, or 97 feet below the capital, and 238 feet higher than Urondogani. In the distance between the capital and Urondogani, there are in the space alluded to no fewer than twelve rivers crossed, including the Luajerri, a wide body of water, sluggish and slow in current, and is said to rise in the Nyanza. From whence or to what point do all these streams flow? We are not told, and cannot make out.

The Katonga River is a large body of water coming from the north-west quarter, and with a slow current flowing into the Nyanza about 50 miles west of the capital. Beyond it there is, almost every quarter of a mile, large " rush-drains " flowing in the same direction. At the mouth of this stream there are forty islands, the largest of which is called Sese, where the king keeps his fleet of canoes. From the mouth of the Katonga coming from north-west to the mouth of the Mwerango, running north-east, is not more than 20 miles. From the mouth of Murchison Creek, by the Kira, a canoe station, to Urondogani, the king's naval commander stated there were nu-

merous shoals, rocks, and great cataracts in the
Nyanza, such as render the navigation dangerous
and almost impracticable. " Boats from Murchison
Creek never visit Kira " (p. 469), which is the most
eastern district of Uganda. From Kira it would take
one month by the lake to go to the Masai country,
where there is another Nyanza to which the king's
canoes go for salt, but the same place could be gained
in seven days, viz., " four by land and three by
water " (p. 429). The passage from Murchison Creek
to Usoga is very circuitous on account of reefs or
shoals. In this route the Kitiri Island is passed (p.
399). The Waganda know of no other Kitiri but
this. It cannot be above 80 miles from their north-
east frontier.

In descending the river from Urondogani we meet
with continued confusion and evidently impracticable
positions. At Kamrasi's palace the distance that is
given to Lake Luta Nzigé is about 70 miles. At the
Karuma Falls we may fairly take the distance to be
the same. The lake in its southern position is given as
2,200 feet above the level of the sea. By what means
or knowledge this elevation was ascertained is not
stated, but we assume it to be correct. The Karuma

Falls, as they are called, having only 10 feet descent, are 2970 feet above the level of the sea. To the lake there is, therefore, a descent of 770 feet in a distance of 60 or 70 miles.

At this point should commence the supposed backwater, of 166 miles in length, towards the S.S.W. But how are we to manage for the subsequent descent of the river beyond the northern point of this lake? To the point where the river is met with beyond Paira, 120 miles from the Karuma Falls, the descent is stated to be 1,000 feet, say (400 feet higher than Gondokoro), and consequently nearly 300 feet below the level of the north point of the Luta Lake. How, then, could the Nile form a backwater from this? This is not thought of, nor explained. The fact is that this backwater expanse was, we believe, made out in London in order to cobble up something like consistency and unity, and also to account for the diminution of the river in magnitude, which they found as they advanced northwards.

Kamrasi, Chief of Unyoro, or, as he is there styled, "King of Kings," has, we think, been very much belied. He has been portrayed as an out-and-

out butcher. Now to us he really appears the best
of the lot. When his subjects offend him he flogs
them, telling them that it is fortunate for them they
have such a merciful sovereign, for if they were
under Mtésa, he would, for the same offence, cut off
their heads. He has eight fattened queens, each of
whom is so large that it takes eight men to raise her
up. His attention to these ladies must occupy so
much of his time that he can have but little to spare
either to do good or to do evil. His domicile is very
simple, containing, besides himself, in one puddle-
hole room, cows, pigs, poultry, and birds, clean and
unclean.

But what is Nyanza, and how much of it, if lake
it be, has been discovered ? The word means equally
" pond," " river," or " lake," and is applied as the
name of the river from Ripon Falls downwards to
Kidi and Gani. All that Speke saw of it was at
Muanza, and only so far as his eyes could carry him.
His next sight was at Mashonde or Makaka, about
20 miles south of the Equator. There he got the
first glimpse of what he supposed to be the lake in
his second journey. He saw no more of it even at
the Ripon Falls, because " the spur of a hill " shut

out his view of seeing the outlet of the Napoleon
Channel. To that point Speke's view of the water
or lake was only about 50 miles out of 450 miles.
All the rest was hearsay.

Captain Speke pointedly informs us that he had
satisfied the King of Uganda "that he knew everything." The king knew better. He succeeded in
detaining him in his palace for five months, yet
within only five hours' walk of what was considered
to be the Nyanza, without permitting him to go to
see it, or getting hold of any one who could give
him a direct answer to plain inquiries made about it.
Captain Speke was all the time mentioned amused
and employed in drinking pombe, courting the
Queen Dowager, shooting cows, reducing to order
his rebellious female inmates, some of whom had
caught the itch from consorting with dirty children,
and in splashing in the Nyanza in company with the
king's naked queens, when not engaged in witness-
ing the execution of some of them. It is almost incredible that any man, but especially a man who had
come one thousand miles to see the position of the
outlet of the Nile, supposed to be in that spot, should
remain five months within eight miles of it, without

hearing or seeing something certain about the great object of his research, or have found some means to see it. Why, he might have taken the arm of the beautiful Kariana, the wife of the courtier Dumba, with whom he was accustomed to walk arm-in-arm to teach her how to walk as he walked with the ladies in Hyde Park, shaved his beard, slipped on his or her Mbugu, and instead of sitting moping and mourning, walked off in a morning walk with Kariana, got to the lake or the river, and so in one forenoon seen what he wanted, and thus relieved us and the world from all our pain and disappointment. We think he might have set some scheme on foot that would have gained his object.

In the first journey we were most pointedly told that no Arab or native merchant or traveller ever crossed the country to the northward of 1° of N. lat. We are, however, now told merchants frequently do so; that the road from Uganda through the Masai country is well known and often frequented, and by it King Mtésa offered to send Speke to the coast in one month. Speke himself appears to have thought of returning to Zanzibar by this route. At page 187 he tells us that Irungu, a native of

Uganda, expressed his surprise that he had come so far about, when he could have taken the short, safe, and well-known route to his country by Masai and Usogo.

Next it may be asked, where are the celebrated Mountains of the Moon ? We have seen how easily and readily the newly-discovered ones have been pushed about. Two reasons may be adduced how and why the old mountains may have got out of the way. First, they had doubtless heard, like everything else, by the boastings of the first expedition, that Indian Englishmen could blow up Africa, and, consequently, these mountains included; and when they heard that Speke had returned, they doubtlessly considered that he had come to execute his object. Looking at matters from this point of view, those lofty hills might consider it proper and prudent to emigrate to some safer quarter—perhaps to the Moon herself—where there has, within the last few years, been discovered a number of very elevated peaks; or the whole, or the remnant that stopped at home, may have disappeared, and been lowered by the following process :—At the extra meeting of the Royal Geographical Society, June 23, 1863 (*Proceed-*

ings vol. vii., p. 221), Captain Speke enraptured the listening throng thus : " The Mountains of the Moon are wearing down, and so is Africa! " Now, as the lake, according to the same authority, had sunk 200 feet in three years, the hills and the land must have done so also. This being so, at the rate of 70 feet decrease per annum, we shall, in 75 years more, find the Mediterranean Sea running by Uganda into the Indian Ocean near Zanzibar, or the Indian Ocean from the latter point, by the same route, flowing into the Mediterranean. This must be the result, or else Speke's beautiful theory must be wholly wrong.

Ptolemy is the first author who brought those mountains before the world, and before entering into such theories it might have been well for many to have considered carefully what Ptolemy really did say on this subject. As many words and opinions have been put into his mouth which he certainly never uttered, so it might happen that he has been misrepresented or misunderstood upon this important subject also ; and that the world, thoughtless as it is known to be, has been hunting after a phantom which has never existed. We accordingly searched out the passage. The expression used appears to us very remarkable. It is " Selenes Oros," " Moon *Mountain*," not *Mountains* of the Moon, as has for ages been stated. But lest we should be mistaken we called the attention of an Oxford scholar to it, and he told us that " Selenes Oros," Moon *Mountain*, in the singular, was the correct reading.

This is important, and in our opinion is intended to designate, not clusters of mountains, but a mountain chain, which divided the waters that flowed to the north and to the south, and also from its extremities to the west and to the east. The extent of this was taken at 10°; and from Kilimanjaro, say 37° E. long., or Kenia in 36° E. long., 10° westward brings us to 27° or 26° E. long.; and in this space we have all the features of Africa, lakes and mountains, alluded to by Ptolemy. That early geographer placed his Lake Nilus a little to the south of the Equator, and 5° E. long. from Alexandria—that is, in 34° or 35° E. long. by our mode of reckoning. He was led into an error in placing these portions of the interior, bearing, as he conceived, from certain points in the east. Thus he places Cape Aromatum (Cape Asser or Cape Guardafui) in 6° N. lat., which we know to be in 11° 48′ 50″, being thus, say 6° out of its true place. He places the lake, the source of the western branch of the river, 1° more to the north and 8° more to the west than the one for the eastern branch; subsequent inquiries may show us that these great eatures of Africa may yet turn out to be substantially correct.

We cannot here enter into any disquisition regarding the discrepancies that appear amongst the very ancient authors regarding these parts of Africa. We notice only those that are consistent and most valuable, and as bearing upon the priority of discovery and geographical knowledge. The earliest period we hear of Ethiopia is in the capture of the capital thereof by Moses 1400 years before our era, and 90 or 100 years before the departure of the Israelites from Egypt. Josephus calls it Saba, and states that it was very strong, situated on the River Astosabos, and that the name was changed to Meroe, by Cambyses, in honour of his sister Meroe. There known to ancient writers three great tributaries to the Nile in Ethiopia, namely, the Astaboras (Tacazze), the Astosabos (Blue River), and the Astapus (White River). Herodotus, 450 years before our era, obtained much information regarding those interior parts of Africa, and in general, in its grand features, pretty correct. He says the source of the Nile, Astosabos, was 20 days' journey to the south of Meroe, which will bring it to the Lake Dembea or Tzana. According to Ptolemy, the position of Meroe was in 16° 25′ N. lat., but the ancient astronomer Hipparchus has placed it in 16° 51′, which may be taken as the most correct. Caillaud found the vast ruins in 16° 56′. Under Psammeticus, the first Egyptian king that reigned after the final expulsion of the Ethiopian kings from Egypt, 240,000 emigrants from Egypt settled in an island south of the island of Meroe, that is beyond Khartoum, between the Blue and the White Rivers, and at eight days' journey east of the Nubœ, or Nubatœ. Those and the adjacent parts must therefore have been well known to the Egyptians. Subsequently the Roman arms extended to those parts. Petronius, the Roman general under Augustus, thirty years before our era, took and destroyed Napata, the ancient capital of Tirhaka, situated on the great northern bend of the Nile at Mount Barkhall, where vast ruins are still found. Meroe certainly, the capital of Queen Candace, mentioned in the New Testament (Acts viii. 27), also fell under the Roman yoke. Nero, early in his reign, sent a remarkable exploring party, under two centurions, with military force, to explore the source of the Nile and the countries to the west of the Astapus or White River, at that early day considered to be the true Nile. Assisted by an Ethiopian sovereign (Candace, no doubt), they went through the district now known as Upper Nubia, to a distance of 890 Roman miles from Meroe. In the last part of their journey they came to immense marshes, the end of which no one seemed to know, amongst which the channels were so narrow that the light boat or canoe in use was barely sufficient to carry one man across them. Still they continued their course south till they saw the river tumbling down or issuing out between two rocks, when they turned back, carrying with them a map of the regions through which they had passed : for Nero's guidance and information. This, it may be remarked, is exactly the case still. The Dutch ladies told us last year that they found the channels amongst these marshes so thick that the lightest canoe, made of bulrushes, scarcely fit to carry one man, could find room to pass on them, or across them. After this, Pliny, Strabo, and other Roman authors, took notice of this portion of Africa, but without giving us anything important or new. Soon after Ptolemy became the chief authority on these subjects, and collected a great deal of useful information elsewhere noticed. After him came the Arabs, who adopted closely all his geographical notions and delineations, which renders it unnecessary to say anything more about them here. It is, however, both pleasing and satisfactory to find those marshes and the rivers as described to us to-day, to be the same—exactly the same—that they were, we may say, 3500 years ago. Eschylus, who wrote 500 years before our era, positively mentions these immense marshes.

No. IV.—GEOGRAPHY, CLIMATE, COM-
MERCE, &c.

We may here make a few references to the Ara-
bian geographers. Belad el Sudan, or country of
the blacks, says Backui, extends on the east to
Ethiopia. Edrisi, who was born in Nubia, but who
wrote in Egypt about A.D. 1400, says, in that part
of Ethiopia south and south-west of Nubia is first
seen the separation of the two Niles. The one
flows from south to north into Egypt, and the other
part of the Nile flows from east to west; and upon
that branch of the Nile lie all, or at least the most
celebrated kingdoms of the Negroes. " From the
Mountains of the Moon," says Scheadeddin, " the
Egyptian Nile takes its rise. It cuts horizontally
the Equator in its course north. Many rivers come
from this mountain, and unite in a great lake.
From this lake comes the Nile, the greatest and
most beautiful of the rivers of all the earth. Many
rivers derived from this great river, water Nubia,
&c.

From the Arabs we may fairly descend to our

own times. The early Portuguese discoverers obtained a great deal of geographical information regarding the interior of Africa, and especially regarding two lakes near the Equator, from one of which, the most northern, the Egyptian Nile was stated to flow. This information was largely used by the French geographer (D'Anville), and the Dutch geographers of that time. Subsequently Bruce and others told us about the great disparity in magnitude between the Blue and the White Rivers; the latter, they asserted, rose far to the south, near to the Equator, and amongst mountains covered with eternal snow. Twenty-five years ago, Mahomed Ali, the clear-sighted and energetic ruler of Egypt, sent an expedition, consisting of several barques, well provided with everything necessary, and under able naval officers, to explore the White Nile to its source, if possible. They did their work so far well, but were forced to return back on the 26th January, 1840, in lat. 3° 22′ N., for want of sufficient depth of water for their vessels. At lat. 3° 30′ they found the river 1,370 feet broad and say six feet deep. In every day's work on the voyage they gave the width of the river, the depth of the river, the force of its current, its temperature, and the miles (geographical) made good daily. Captain Speke will surely remember that the official account of this voyage was put into his hands after his return from his first African journey, showing from it that the Egyptian officers had advanced a few miles beyond the north termination (3° 30' N.) of his lake. He has now found out the truth of this exploration, but which he and other wiseacres at the time treated with derision. Nobody, says he, then believed it. Since then, Dr. Peney and M. Miani have gone up the stream to about 3° N. lat., and M. Vincent Angelo, a German missionary, ascended beyond 2° N. lat. His account has been confirmed by Captain Speke, who tells us (p. 507), that in passing down the river he saw, when in 1° 40' N. lat., Mount Udongo, the Padongo of Angelo, to the east of his course. The Church Missionary Society's excellent missionaries had before this time made us acquainted with the source of a river in a lake near to, but west of Mount Kenia, about 80 miles east of Speke's new source, from which a river flowed N.W. to Massr (Egypt). The Dutch ladies confirm the accuracy of the turning-point of the Egyptian expedition, where they state they steamed beyond Gondokoro, six or eight hours in time. Arab traders worthy of credit had also informed us of Speke's Nyanza and its position; in short, only a small space of country actually remained to be explored—explored, not to be discovered—when Speke went upon his first journey. His boast, therefore, made at Taunton, Dec. 24, 1863, as the real discoverer, that he "had in 1857 hit the Nile on the head, and in 1863 drove it down to the Mediterranean," is greatly inaccurate. Moreover, no mortal man should make such a boast. Here also Speke meets with a previous discoverer. We quote from a volume which we always delight to look into, and the authority of which cannot be impugned. There we find that, 600 years before our era, a haughty Egyptian king, for himself and for Egypt, told the world thus:—"My river is mine own, and I have made it for myself." Of course he must have known every part of the Nile, from its head to its mouth. But what is the reply of Omnipotence? "I will make it (Egypt) a base kingdom; it shall be the basest of the kingdoms (slaves to slaves); neither shall it

exalt itself any more above the nations." (*Ezek.*
c. xxix., v. 2, 3, 15.) Is it not so? Has it not
always been so, since that decree was pronounced?
To Speke we would say, "Be not high-minded, but
fear."

Numerous remarkable theories have been advanced regarding the sources and the course of the
Nile, both in ancient and in modern times. It was
stated to be the Gihon of Paradise, and to run round
Arabia, and again to come from Hindostan, running
under the sea till it came to the middle of Africa,
south of the Mountains of the Moon, then supposed to be in about 10° S. lat. At that point,
according to Mela, it sprang up a river at the
edge of the land, and thence descended north as the
river of Egypt. Herodotus and some Roman
authors joined to it the streams descending from
Mount Atlas, and carried it through Africa to the
Nile, and as forming the parent stream of that river.
Such, too, was for a long time the opinion of some
more modern writers. The late Sir John Barrow
adopted this opinion, and carried the Niger and the
Nile, as one, to the White River above Khartoum.
The geographers on the other side of the Channel,

not many years ago, took up the stream in the Bahr el Ghazal, at Lake Tchad, and carried it over hill and dale by the now so-called Bahr el Ghazal to the White River. The word Bahr el Ghazal means simply a swampy, marshy, occasionally inundated district of country. Hence the error and confusion that took place, and is even at this moment continued. About thirty years ago, two East Indian naval officers, Smee and Hardy, seeing the Luffia on the east coast when it was in full flood, set it down as the veritable Niger of Timbuctoo. We could swell this list of strange opinions about the Nile, but it would be a waste of time to do so.

Next, we must here allude to Speke's wonderful Hindoo map (p. 23) of the Nile. That Hindostan had much communication with Eastern Africa is well known, but with Europe communication only began by way of the Red Sea shortly before the reign of Justinian. After the Arab conquest the trade between Eastern Africa and India was greatly increased; but these people closely adopted the geography of Ptolemy as their guide in that line of communication. Whoever takes the trouble to look at the map which Speke has produced as something marvellous and to us wholly new, will perceive at a glance that it is Ptolemaic and Arabic authority which has been followed. Thus it places the south end or head of this river lake in 12° S. lat., the very parallel where Ptolemy has erroneously placed it. To this error Speke's absurdity has to be added, which is, that he turns the whole upside down. He calls it Amara, or Lake of the Gods. Amara, according to several authorities—and amongst those is Speke himself—is not far from the Equator, and Uganda the place of old Jupiter's Ethiopian winter retreat. Rapta, in this precious map, is placed at the south head of the lake, and far inland, whereas Rhaptum, or Rapta, as Speke has it, is a remarkable promontory on the sea coast in East Africa, supposed to be near Zanzibar. It is thus the misfortune of our author that when he gets hold of anything new, so to misplace it as to render it useless to himself or any one else. Besides this, we are informed on good authority, that this map is a fabrication by an authority whose name we have forgotten.

Beyond Usoga, and Ukori, and Amara, Speke expressly tells lay the Galla (p. 383) country. But this fact has long been known. This great African people are spread over a large portion of Africa, and are quite distinct from the Abyssinians. The Great Lake was situated in their country, which, they said, was so large that a vulture took three hours to fly over it. In the maps constructed by De Lisle for Louis XV. of France, this lake is placed reaching north to the Equator, and very nearly indeed where Lake Nyanza is now placed. It was also represented to be studded with islands. The dominion of the Galla extended to the parallel of 8° lat. on the south, and to the meridian of 29° E. long. on the west, or perhaps even farther. Their territories are, however, now much restricted. Still their numbers are at present estimated at 5,000,000, all of whom Roman Catholic missionaries say they have converted to their Church. When they first attacked Abyssinia they came from the south, and were considered to be an African tribe. Those who inhabited the hilly districts in the interior were represented as almost white. Bruce saw one from the neighbourhood of the Equator and the lake who was perfectly white. When the power of these people came to be much restricted in Eastern Africa, some of their chiefs no doubt remained in the most distant western parts of their former possessions, and obtained power and authority over the rude native tribes, and it is probable that the progeny of those chiefs are there still, remaining in the countries where Speke found his superior race of men, and of whose fine daughters he was so greatly enamoured. The ancient and even the present Gallas had many cruel customs, and which much resembled some that prevailed in Palestine, Phœnicia, and some parts of Western Asia. They were the Huns and Tartars of Africa. Ruin and desolation marked their progress everywhere. They had no connection with Abyssinia. Sir William C. Harris mentions a report that they came from Arabia into Eastern Africa in very remote times. Still they have been by many considered an indigenous African race.

Captain Speke informs us that he most strenuously taught his Wahuma friends in Karagwe and Uganda that they ought to reverence deeply the great river, the head of which was within their dominions, because in Egypt, to which it descended, " it had cradled (p. 467) the first expounder (Moses) of our religious belief, or Christianity; which Christianity, Europe having embraced, had in its practice rendered its people superior to the people in every other quarter of the world."

Now we have ever believed, and been taught to believe, that the origin and base of Christianity was in that immutable judgment pronounced by the Judge of All in the Garden of Eden, when he told the enemy of mankind that " the seed of the woman" whom he had deceived should " crush his head."

It was this doctrine and religion that Adam taught his children, that Noah preached, that Abraham was promised and was glad to learn, that Moses typified and taught, that strung King David's lyre, that inspired Isaiah's tongue, and that which the heavenly hosts assembled on Bethlehem's plains attested, and came down to attest, on that hallowed night when they proclaimed to angels and men the advent of Him who came to carry out in his own good time and way the terrible, the immutable decree. Captain Speke should really make himself better acquainted with these sacred subjects before he ventures upon them.

Again, we are told by our author that Japhet was

white. This is not new in history, though some of his descendants (the Mongols and Tartars) are dusky enough. Shem was tawny, and Ham's progeny were black, and that these were to continue under Noah's curse till he (Speke) came "to regenerate" Africa. Ham's progeny were very numerous. One portion of them emigrated, or were driven in process of time, from Shinar into Hindostan; another portion, by a similar process, were driven into Africa. But all Ham's progeny were not blacks. The Canaanites, Hivites, &c., were not so; neither were the ancient Egyptians. The progeny of Shem were all fair, not tawny—Persians, Medes, Babylonians, Chaldeans, Syrians, Arabians, and Hebrews, both male and female. Shem* means especially name, likeness, image, and is often applied in Scripture to designate the Second Person in the Holy Trinity. Its meaning, therefore, in the son of Noah, is the image or likeness of the first, and also of the second Adam. Japhet was no doubt white. The Hebrew verb or name means "to persuade," and has certainly a prophetic meaning. Hence it is said,

* See Parkhurst on the word Shem.—"Name, fame, renown, reputation. Name is the representative of a being or a thing," &c.

" God shall persuade Japhet, and he shall dwell in the tents of Shem." This clearly means that they should become one family, which dwelling in the same tents means, and which the emphatic and figurative Eastern expression always conveys. Such Japhet's progeny are daily becoming, and such they will completely be when they all become Christians. How much of Japhet's blood may be infused into Speke's veins we know not; he has not stated, nor is it of any consequence to inquire into. Besides, we cannot comprehend what object Speke has in view by introducing Adam and Noah into his system relating to the manner in which change of colour is produced by mixing the blood of mankind. Neither of the names mentioned did, or could possibly do so.

The sexes mix and will continue to mix. Different colours will follow. Captain Speke is himself a most competent witness as to the process. Every one who has been in India and in the western tropical world knows how Japhet can be made black, Ham white, and Shem tawny. It may begin by a kind of douce violence, or beguiling by the soft arts of love, as it were, and proceed onward as follows. The reader will remember the royal pombe banquet at which Speke was the favoured guest. When the uproarious party broke up, he told the Queen Dowager that " he admired her wisdom ;" that " though his feet might drag his body away from her, his heart would still remain here, for he loved her much." Our author must have been more than half seas over when he spoke thus ; in short,

> " In the trough, uproarious,
> O'er all the ills of life victorious."

When the great prince returns to Uganda, he will be able to tell if there are more people there than formerly that are " half black and half white ;" and if on one head there is seen hair like Speke's and any of Nyanamore's family. But why the sacred names of Adam, Noah, and Moses should be dragged into such a mass of rubbish, we cannot understand. Even as a " succour dodge," it will not avail the arguments and theories of our author.*

* Here we may point out the difference in taste between different travellers. When the African chiefs sent Du Chaillu the finest young women they could select " to carry his water," he always returned them indignantly, and chose as his " maid-of-

Our author is again very greatly at fault in what he states regarding Dr. Krapf. This gentleman never said that a salt lake existed near or at Mount Kenia. What Dr. Krapf stated was, that near, and west of Mount Kenia, there was a lake from which issued a river that ran to Massr or Egypt. It was Mr. Erhardt who subsequently stated that, according to report, a large salt-water lake, called Baharingo, was found a little to the north of the Equator. He did not say that the lake in question had any outlet; and still less that a fresh-water river came from it. This point of belief he left to theorists and credulous people like Captain Speke to propagate and to credit. But in this portion of Africa we now know that there is no lake, salt or fresh, but an undulating country, with natron wells from which salt is obtained. In reference also to what is taken as salt-water lakes in this and other parts of Africa, it is well known that on the marshy banks of lakes

all-work" the ugliest old negro female he could find. But our author, whenever an aged or indifferent lass was sent him "to carry his water," invariably sent her back, and insisted that they should send him the youngest and the most handsome they had. He always gained his point, although he was sometimes obliged to "wait a bit" before the better was forthcoming.

and rivers salt is produced from a plant resembling parsley. It is first steeped in water, then the juice expressed and boiled down, when a small quantity of very fine white salt is obtained, but not of great strength. It is sold into adjoining districts, and hence the origin of the stories about salt lakes in some parts of Africa.

In descending the river from Madi by Gondokoro, Speke gives nothing that is new; or, indeed, anything of the slightest consequence. He simply states regarding the important river Sobat, that its middle mouth lies in 9° 20′ 48″ N. lat., and in 31° 24′ 9″ E. long. D'Arnaud places it in 9° 11′ N. lat., and 28° 13′ E. long. from Paris, or in 30° 34′ E. long. from Greenwich. This shows a difference of 11′ lat. and 50′ long. Which is right, or which is wrong, we do not here take upon ourselves to decide.

About the wretched kingdoms in that portion of Africa regarding which such bombastic stories have been given, we may observe that none of them cover a space of 70 square miles, and in each of them rebellions occur probably monthly. Of Mtésa's tyranny we have elsewhere given striking instances. One more, and we have done:—Bombay, Speke's considerate messenger, found that savage king just going to hack four women to death with his own hand. He gave Bombay one of the number, and then urged Bombay to stop and witness "some good sport," while he hacked to pieces the rest. This, Bombay properly declined to do. Yet this is the man, and these are the people, whom Speke taught Sir Roderick Murchison to believe were "the French of these parts, from their sprightliness, and good taste, and behaviour."—(Address, Royal Geographical Society, May 25th, 1863). What shall we hear next? We presume that this state of things is what Speke calls "the germ of Christianity" that remains among those tribes.

Our French friends will scarcely thank Speke for this comparison and intended compliment. Let us now shortly give the account of a Royal marriage. In this instance there were only three brides, but sometimes there are thirty or more so married. The naked damsels were ordered by a female attendant to move on (p. 434); the king commenced a series of huggings, first sitting on the lap of one, whom he clasped to his bosom, crossing his neck with hers, now to the right and then to the left;

and having finished with her, took post on the second one's lap, and then on that of the third, performing on each of them the same evolutions. He then returned to his original position, and the marriage ceremony was supposed to be concluded. This is getting into the palace. Next comes the way that women (wives) get out of it. The same day four women were dragged from the palace for execution, each led by a rope fastened to them and the hands of the executioners. Dragged to a certain spot, the neck of each is dislocated by a blow from a heavy club from behind, the head severed off by a sharp-edged grass, a slow and cruel process; and after other unfeeling barbarities, the corpse left to the vultures or thrown into the lake. Every day one, two, three, and four victims are thus disposed of, being at the rate of at least 1,000 per annum, besides those that are slaughtered in the palace by the king, when he mixes a little business with pleasure, himself or his pages. What would our Parisian friends say if they saw such numbers of young females dragged from the Tuileries, executed, and then their remains thrown into the Seine? Yet the perpetrators of similar atrocities in Uganda are held up to us by Speke as worthy of admiration and respect (p. 389) ! !

In reference to the head of the Nile, or of any other river, we must observe that it is not always the largest branch that gives the name. The Blue River, clearly the smaller stream, has, in this instance, given the name. So also the Mississippi, although its western tributary, the Missouri, is double its length, before their junction takes place, retains the name. So also in our country, on a small scale. In the Clyde, the mountain stream that gives the name is not half the length or the magnitude of the Daea, at their junction in the head of Lanarkshire.

Neither can any lake be taken as the head of a river, though the river may issue from it. Lake Baikal is not the head of the Yenessie River. Lake Tzana is not the head of the Blue River, Lake Dibbie is not the head of the Niger, Lake Geneva not the head of the Rhone, Lake Lausanne not the head of the Rhine, Lake Superior not the head of the St. Lawrence, nor Lake Winnipeg the head of the Sasketchawan, and so of other rivers on this globe; nor is any great lake the sure sign, as Speke says of the Nyanza, of its being the head of a great river; but frequently the reverse. Take for instance, Lake Tchad, Lake Koki Nor, Lake Durah, Lake Van, Lake Nicaragua, Lake Titicaca, &c. Here Captain Speke is again at fault, both in his theory and opinion.

In reference to the true source of what is now considered as the River Nile, where is that, and has Captain Speke discovered it? The answer must decidedly be, CERTAINLY NOT, nor is it nor can it be where he has on second thoughts placed it, the miserable gully the Jordans, in which there is not one drop of fresh water except what comes from the clouds during the rains and from the overflowing of the lake adjoining. On the part of old Nilus we enter the most solemn and determined protest against such an absurd and thoughtless decision. Is it possible, we say, that after the venerable old gentleman has buried his head for 3,500 years from the general knowledge of the world, that it should be suffered to be dug up in a place where there is not a drop of spring water to wet and cool his aged and parched lips? Such degradation cannot be allowed in a river god so famous. We are, therefore, grateful to our facetious contemporary *Punch*, for having given us something more rational, by exhibiting to our eyes, in his own droll way, the source of the Nile in a large body of water, flowing in a copious stream through two large draining-tiles, pushed under the adjoining rocks, with Speke, for so we take it to be, as the deity of the place, sitting calmly smoking his Turkish pipe, a present no doubt from the Dowager Queen of Uganda! This is surely a better and more appropriate source than Speke's; the Old Man will at least get a draught of pure water.

But let us examine this most important point seriously and more fully. In Africa, and also since his return to England, Captain Speke has stated his decided conviction and belief to be, that this Nyanza receives its chief supply of water from the westward by the river Kitangule, and some other rivers. This river he gives near the lake to be 80 yards broad, 14 feet or more deep, with a current at the rate of four miles per hour (p. 261); and this, too, in the dry season. Now, this is a large river. The volume of water passing through any given channel is as the square of the velocity, so that such stream, flowing at the rate of one mile per hour, would, with the depth and current stated, spread to a breadth of 1300 feet. Its chief supplies, doubtless, come from the New Mountains of the Moon, amongst which is Mount Mfumbiro, 10,000 feet high. How this was ascertained is not stated ; but if snow and hail were, as he was told, constantly falling upon it, then it must be much higher, rising even above 17,000 feet, and also at a much greater distance to the westward than where he has placed it.

Again, we are told emphatically that the lake first seen inundates during the rains the districts in the south very extensively. Is it possible that the lake at the north side, which has, in the short space of 30 geographical miles, no fewer than six large outlets running north, can be the same lake, or connected with that sheet of water seen 160 miles to the south ; or from whence can that water come that feeds that which supplies so many streams running northward? Not, certainly, from the Jordans gully ; but should it be so, then it is the only phenomenon of the kind to be seen in any quarter of the globe. The Kitangule river alone cannot possibly give the requisite supply.

The south portion of the lake, Captain Speke tells us, appears to be of little depth, more resembling flooded land than a deep, silent lake. Next, as regards the sources. North of the parallel of Tanganyika, the rainy season commences in November and terminates in the middle of May. Whence could the water come that swelled the Malagarazi river and inundated its banks on the 9th of June, as the travellers found on their return from the lake to Kazeh? It must have come from the north-east, if not from the Muanza Lake. Again, we are told that on the northern shore of the lake the dry season commences in December and terminates in March. This, also, is the case in all the interior districts northwards to Gondokoro. Next, at Ripon Falls, July 23rd, and thence along the river to Kidi, but especially about Kamrasi's palace (Sept. 8th), thence downwards to the Karuma Falls, on Sept. 8th, the Kafu was bringing down numerous floating islands; and from Sept. 8th to the end of October (p. 557—571), both the Kafu and the Nile were constantly rising, bringing down in the stream floating islands, composed of rush, grass, ferns, &c. The rivers they considered to be in full flood, and which flood they also considered they had carried with them, going northwards, since July 23rd to November 9th. When at Karuma Falls they found, as they considered, "the Nile to be in full flood." All this flood is clearly within the time of the regular rains of the northern torrid zone, and has nothing connected with the southern zone. Such islands could scarcely exist and be detached from the shores of a wide lake, unless that lake had been much swollen by the same sphere of rain that had tended to swell the rivers, but which we find fall very lightly in Uganda during December, January, and February (Introduction, p. xvi.). The phenomena here alluded to appear in all tropical rivers.

These points considered, brings us to believe that in the large space (160 miles) between Muanza in the south and Kira in the north, there may really be two distinct lakes; the northern, fed by rivers from the distant west, and the southern by smaller streams from the southward. All Captain Speke's descriptions of the north coast of the lake apply more to the channel and course of a river than to the bed of a lake. This river, suppose it to be so, will resemble greatly some of the rivers in the table-land of British North America, alternately widening and contracting, communicating and interlocking with each other in the secondary lakes, so that they form a network, in short, of rivers, or branches of rivers and smaller lakes, with small rapids between. But this is quite different from a river, large or small, entering and forming a lake, and then issuing from it again in one or more streams ; and it is, moreover, totally different in its nature from the lake situated in the watershed of a country sending off a stream on each side to flow in opposite directions. Besides, the table-lands in British North America, where such inland communications exist, are seldom more than 1,600 to 1,800 feet above the level of the sea, and not very far from it, while this portion of African table-land is nearly 4,000 feet above the level of the sea, and at a great distance from it. But we cannot at this moment go into this subject fully.

Further, Captain Speke pointedly tells us he was satisfied that in Uganda the whole lake, at no very distant period of time, had been upwards of 300 feet higher than it is at present—then extending over the districts of Unyoro, Uganda, and part of Karagwe. What, then, becomes of the districts on the south side, which are not stated to have been disturbed? These must have been 600 or 800 feet below the lake.

Had Captain Speke been acquainted with, or allowed himself to have been fully acquainted with the researches of others that had preceded him in Eastern Africa, he might, even with the rambling data which he has gleaned, have made out a more rational delineation of this portion of Africa than he has done. On the contrary, he has left everything indefinite, confused, and unsatisfactory. Take, for instance, the important position of Kira. At page 449 he informs us that it was a Royal boat station on the Nyanza, on the road to Urondogani by the Nyanza. At page 472 he tells us that he was at Kira, from which place he despatched a messenger to King Mtésa; yet not a word he tells us of what he saw at Kira, or about either lake or river. No correct or thinking geographer can find his way in such pages. It would puzzle the most acute Philadelphia lawyer to unravel the maze, or to derange the narrative more than Captain Speke himself has done.

In reference to the climate of this portion of

Africa, and that its great salubrity is well adapted to European constitutions, we totally, and from some knowledge of tropical climates, dissent from it. The hills of Karagwe may be comparatively healthy, but the valleys must be hot and moist, both of which are inimical to health, especially to Europeans. Along the whole northern shore of the lake to Napoleon Inlet the country is comparatively flat, intersected with deep gullies and drains, stagnant pools, or nearly stagnant waters, numerous marshes, streams covered thickly with water plants and long grass, perhaps six feet in height. Towards Kidi, northwards, and in the surrounding country, swamp and jungle are the masters of the situation, and almost banish human beings from the countries around. In Kidi the jungle is extensive and terrific ; and between Karagwe and Uganda a large space of country is totally uninhabited. With the whole country undrained, the thermometer ranging from 60° to 90°, according to the season or the time of the day, it is impossible that such districts can be suitable for or suited to European constitutions.

With regard to the great question of commerce, we remark, did it never strike Captain Speke in his advance,—declaring, as he frequently and emphatically did, that he went to open up an entirely new channel,—that the jealous tribes to the south of the lake would see in that the ruin of their present trade, and thus render them unfriendly to his object? As regards the chiefs to the northward, could he not perceive that the chiefs of Karagwe would in his Nile project see the priority preference as to profit and revenue given to Mtésa by placing him before them, and Kamrasi of Unyoro before both? They dreaded this, and accordingly he is obliged to tell us that his kind friend Rumanika had sent secret instructions to Mtésa to show him little or nothing in Uganda, and when he had finished with him, to send him (Speke) back to Uganda, to perfect, perhaps, his engineering skill upon his fatted Queens. But truly, the idea of any settled or profitable commerce between these parts of Africa and Europe is a complete delusion. In remote regions such as these, where there is no stable government, whether legitimate or usurped, and no recognised and just laws, and where there is and can be no security for life, liberty, and property,—because, as Kamrasi told Speke, on the death of a ruler, by natural death or violence, the legitimate successor or daring rebel and usurper fought for the regal dignity, the strongest, of course, being the successful ruler,—in such countries no security can be found. Besides, where are the roads or easy means of communication, either by land or by water? There are none whatever. The population everywhere are poor, miserable, plundered, enslaved, and engaged in perpetual wars. In every tribe and state also the population are all either averse to continuous labour, or to any labour at all calculated to produce or collect any quantity of tropical produce for exchange, either for internal or external trade. The uncertainty, length, and danger of internal conveyance are everywhere so great, that even if such articles as sugar, coffee, or cotton could be obtained for nothing, none of these articles would defray the cost of bringing them from distant interior parts to the sea-coast for any European or Asiatic market. Can industry and commerce, which must always go hand in hand, exist in such countries? No.

Captain Speke informs us, that when in Karagwe he dreamed that he was actively engaged with Sir Roderick Murchison in devising a plan for an expedition to cross Africa from sea to sea, and, of course, to regenerate Africa. It appears, from what has since occurred, that he intends to do so. At Taunton he dwelt upon his gigantic project, but whether Sir Roderick will join in the scheme or not time will show. "My object is," says he, "nothing less than to regenerate Africa." For this purpose he selects districts near the Equator, "where only three inches of rain fall each day." In addition to the negro clergy there ought to be Ambassadors to Africa, men with authority from our Government, and who, trading with the kings (British Ambassadors trading with kings!), would be also a first step to put an end to the diabolical slave trade.

The direct plan of doing this would be by organising an expedition in the following way:—In the first place let there be negro depôts along the east and the west coasts of Africa, assisting emancipated slaves. Let these be trained as sailors and taught the English language, so that they may assist our own navigators. Let these natives be taken across the continent of Africa and shown the positions in which the trade chiefly exists, and then prevent the merchants conveying slaves. After the depôts had been formed I would take in the aggregate five hundred men, a few from each station, and would then commence from the east coast of Africa and march across along the Equator to the west coast. "The negroes, or blacks, cannot rule their own land, therefore to rule it well there must be a government therein like the British Government in India." "I will engage in it myself if the Government feel inclined to support me in it."

To this wild project even the Prime Minister of the King of Uganda would properly exclaim (see page 279) "Woh, woh, woh, what will happen next?" If our Prime Minister whenever such a scheme is laid before him does not meet it with a similar shout, we are greatly mistaken, and will then, and then only, if he does not so consider it, believe that he has lost all knowledge of geography, which we know he formerly possessed, and all knowledge of mankind, their affairs and objects, which he is known to possess in such an eminent degree.

However, in the present state of wild feeling which predominates in this country, there is no saying what may take place. The very magnitude of the expenditure such an impracticable scheme would require to carry out, will probably secure the trial of it. The idea, however, of carrying negroes trained as navigators on the East Coast of Africa to the West Coast of that continent, through the whole interior of the continent, instead of conveying them by sea by the way of the Cape of Good Hope, is so novel and would be so expensive that it is sure to find supporters in this wealthy and easily-deluded country. Judging from the expenditure incurred in Captain Speke's late expedition (probably 7,000*l.*, including his expenses in Egypt and passage thence to this country, and all Baker's), a few hundreds of thousands of pounds would go but a little way to defray the " preliminary expenses " in the pursuit of this gigantic *ignis fatuus*, while the future expenditure of many many millions would certainly give full scope to numerous gigantic jobs, yielding a profitable return to the projectors and the supporters of the scheme.

If Sir Roderick Murchison takes our sincere and humble advice he will have nothing to do with this new African " dream." But as some one may probably be sent back, we would earnestly implore both the Royal Geographical Society and the

Government to take especial care regarding those who are to be sent on the important work. They must not patronise or send—

First. Such men as seek to make capital for themselves, not wealth for Africa, by tales about the slave trade and cotton.

Secondly. They must not send such men as make, and have made it their sport, to murder elephants. Those creatures may be rendered serviceable to man, and, moreover, appear to have more judgment than a large majority of the people of Africa and other bipeds who visit her unhappy shores : and

Thirdly. They must not send men, if such men there be, who "kiss and tell," and then boast that they do so.

No such men will ever regenerate Africa. There is, however, one man who has been strangely kept in the background in the late journeys—Captain Grant—"throughout the gentleman." He would suit, providing he accepts the task ; to be accompanied by associates, but, with the above exceptions, of his own choosing. We never find him engaged in drinking pombe, flirting or coquetting, and collecting harems. Even when dancing with Ukulima

(p. 138) he is the gentleman, and with that character, bows kindly towards the drooping and delighted creature. He is the man; he will not, we think, waste his time in anything nonsensical.

We have said that the true Nile source has not yet been found out. Well, there are others who also think as we do, for just as we were finishing our wearisome and painful task, a letter from Baker to Consul Petherick, dated March 9th, 1863, came into our hands, in which he says he had determined " to devote twelve months to the discovery of the Nile sources." So these remain still to be discovered! Wonders succeed wonders, for he goes on to say, " there should be a public-house built on the equator, where the traveller could obtain a glass of beer. It will become a great highway—a fashionable tour." Well, by all means let us have the hotel, say thus:—

THE RIPON FALLS HOTEL.

SPEKE AND MTÉSA.

Pombe and Mbugus Always Ready.

If such an establishment is proposed under a Royal charter, which the Government could not refuse, we will bet a new English penny coin against a royal Mbugu that the requisite capital would be obtained amongst the multitudes in this country whose heads are softer than their hearts. A hotel, a splendid Court, where flirting, intriguing, and drinking pombe are the order of the day, would be sure to draw a fashionable array of visitors, as a railway will follow.

There are always two sides to a story, whatever that story may be. We can, however, give at once both sides of the tale we are about to notice, differing as they very widely do. At page 607 Captain Speke tells us that " though I was much annoyed at Petherick, yet I did not wish to break friendship, but dined and conversed with him." Of this, the only dinner, an eye-witness (Mrs. Petherick), in a letter dated Khartoum, December 21st, 1863, most pointedly tells us that Petherick's boats with ample supplies had reached Gondokoro before Baker's, and also before Speke came up; with Baker's assent she made out a list of proper necessaries for them (we have already seen what those were). They were all packed up, sent, and returned, with Speke's thanks for the attention paid, but adding that Baker had already packed and furnished supplies. Our space prevents us from noticing at length those strange occurrences :—

'But they (Speke and Baker) dined with us, and we had a tremendously large ham, which we had brought from England, cooked. This we always said should be done when we met Speke. During dinner I endeavoured to prevail on Speke to accept our aid, but he drawlingly replied, "I do not wish to recognise the succour dodge." The rest of the conversation I am not well enough to repeat. I grow heart-sick now as I did then. After all our toil! Never mind, it will recoil upon him yet, his heartless conduct. I soon left the table, and never dined with them again.'

But this is but a trifling portion of the narrative. It is surpassed by the effrontery of what follows. In a letter from Speke, dated April 19th, 1863, written in the British Consulate (Petherick was then British Consul) at Khartoum, on his way down the river to "my dear Petherick," he proceeds thus :—

'We came down the Nile all right, the last Nigger arriving on the fortieth day, and have lived ever since very comfortably under the tender care of

your fair Fatima.* To-morrow we hope to be well
away in the early morning, consigning your small
packages to their destination in as good order as
you gave them to us. The spades you gave us I
have made over to Fatty, as our Reis bought sheep
on the way with dollars. I was sorry to find, on
arrival here, that the townspeople had reported you
dead, and in consequence of it the Royal Geographical Society had determined on sending the second
thousand pounds to Baker, with a view to assist in
looking after us. This now is too bad; for Habil
never gave the slightest credence to the report
brought down by the merchants, and stated so in
his answers to his brother's inquiries at Cairo. To
make the best of the matter, and to do justice to all,
I wrote home a full explanation of our conversations
at home before we left England, and the position we
were in at Gondokoro. Should you feel inclined to
write a full statement of the difficulties you had to
contend with in going up the White Nile, it would

---

* This fair Fatima was Petherick's cook. Speke has sent her
his photograph : but what else the "great prince" gave her from
his royal bounty, for all her tender care, he saith not ; which is
somewhat surprising.

be a great relief to the mind of every person connected with the succouring fund, and also to myself, as people's tongues are always ready in this meddling world. With Grant's best wishes conjointly with my own to Mrs. Petherick and yourself for your health and safety in the far interior, believe me, yours truly.'

Well, Speke's mind will be speedily relieved. Petherick's full report was to leave Khartoum about the close of December. Scarcely any human being, but especially female, could have survived the miseries that Mrs. Petherick has endured. Yet this heroic lady concludes thus:—"With nothing to conceal and no action to blush for, no wrong done to any one, we patiently wait the result." Justice will at last arrive. Then the great Indian Prince must descend from his Musned and become like other mortals. " *Magna est veritas et prevalebit.*"

No. V.—CONCLUSION.

THE length to which our observations on this subject extended in our previous numbers induced us to stop where we did. But on recurring to the question, and in reviewing what we had done, we found that several important points and facts requisite to elucidate more fully and clearly the whole subject had been omitted. We proceed, and as concisely as possible, to revert to these—to authorities both ancient and modern.

In reference to the important river, Sobat or Red River (which is the meaning of the word), we simply gave Speke's longitude and latitude of it, according to his middle mouth, to contrast with those given by M. Arnaud, and without any further remark. There is no such a thing as three mouths for this river; it has only one, by which Mahomed Ali's expedition entered, and went up it about 150 miles. At the point where they turned back the officers found the stream 1100 feet broad and 12 feet deep, with a current at the rate of one half-mile per hour, and this in the height of the dry season. They considered the river to bring down a moiety of the water of the Nile. Captain Speke, in his celebrated oration on his first appearance in the Geographical Society after his return, and also in his statement inserted in the *Proceedings of the Royal Geographical Society*, vol. vii., p. 223, states that the River Sobat, and one that he calls Giraffe, run into the Blue River after a "graceful sweep," and not into the White River. His words are, "The Blue River combining with the Giraffe and Sobat describes a graceful sweep. In the height of the dry season on the White River, the Blue River is found navigable owing to the great accessions of the Giraffe and Sobat rivers." It is not worth our while to point out the quarter from whence Speke borrowed this and three mouths to the Sobat. But as Petherick's journals and observations are now in the hands of the Royal Geographical Society, we feel confident that these, as regards the Sobat, will confirm the accuracy of the Egyptian expedition account thereof as seen in 1840.[*] The river, we may fur-

---

[*] A letter from Petherick, dated January 12, 1864, just come into our hands, tells what we anticipated. He says, "I was sorry I could not send the measurement of the second Sobat, as I only knew of its existence in the imagination of Captain Speke.

ther observe, instead of no one knowing, as Speke says, where it comes from, is, according to Dr. Peney, found to be a considerable stream about 60 miles east of the Nile, in about 4° N. lat., near the mountains of Leria, not " Illyria," as Speke has it, and there descending from the southward.

Captain Speke gives us no information whatever regarding the Nile, from Gondokoro to Khartoum, either as regards its magnitude, breadth, depth, or current, or the longitudes and latitudes of its more important parts. This is a great want and a grave neglect; nor does he give us any correct idea in all these essential points regarding the river, we may say from the Karuma Falls downwards to Gondokoro, except just to state shortly that near Paira, where they fell in with it north of Faloro, it had there the appearance of " a fine Highland stream," none of which that we know of are in their early sources of any great magnitude. Here, in beholding it as such, they felt surprised at its reduced magnitude when compared to the size they deemed it to be when first seen at Urondogani, namely, 600 to 700 yards in breadth, and very deep, but with a slow current. With regard to the diminished magnitude of the stream at Paira, as compared with that at Urondogani, the solution is easy, because when they saw it at the latter place it was in the rising flood, and at the former, in the height, it may be said, of the dry season. Turning to Dr. Peney, he tells us (*Bulletin*, Paris, 1863) that at the village of Tambour, just in the rapid of Makedo, he found the Nile 45 mètres (190 feet) broad and 19 feet deep, and with a current of nearly eight miles per hour in the centre of the stream. This was at the close of February, in the height of the dry season. The same authority tells us that the Nile rises above six mètres (23 feet) at Gondokoro, and that at this place it is 400 mètres (1594 feet) broad.

It may fairly be presumed that it was on this portion of the Nile that the Centurions of Nero were compelled to turn back. At 600 Roman miles above Meroe they came to the dreadful marshes; but they penetrated to 800 miles (one account says 890 miles), at which distance they must have reached the cataracts and rapids (about 4° N. lat.) on the river, which are found in the quarter which we have just examined. It is, indeed, most remarkable how the discoveries of to-day bear out the accuracy of the descriptions of this quarter of Africa, made, we may say, 3,000 years ago, and showing most clearly that the features and elevation of the country are in every respect the same, thus proving that the great laws of nature which regulate the floods of the Nile remain unaltered. The Nile now begins to rise at Cairo, in Egypt, on the 18th of June, exactly to a day as it did since the oldest period of history, whether sacred or profane, states it to have done.

Here let us correct an error that we had fallen into in the early portion of our review. It was not Debono, reported to be a Maltese, and consequently a British subject, but a nephew of his, that Consul Petherick detected carrying on the slave trade on the White Nile, and sent to Cairo to the British Consul-General to answer for his misdeeds; but perhaps his being a Turkish subject, and one of this privileged class, set him free from any punishment.

Our author, with a dictatorial authority worthy of Mtésa himself, asserts that all the knowledge which the whole progeny of his ancestor Japhet possessed, Greek, Roman, Macedonian, &c., was first taught by and derived from Hindostan. That the whole of these geographers first alluded to, Ptolemy especially, were a set of "humbugs." Now, this is rather hard upon old Ptolemy, after he has placed a lake as the source of the chief branch of the Nile almost upon the exact spot where a lake and the source are placed by Captain Speke. We have already noticed the error which Ptolemy was led into by placing his chief Nile lake due west from a given point on the east coast, while that point was in reality 6° more to the north than he was taught to believe it really was. Again, he places Alexandria in 60° 30′ E. long. from his first meridian, always taken in the westernmost of the Canary Islands — Ferro, in longitude (by our reckoning) 17° 54′ west. This shows an error of 12° 41′ too much. But this error is at once rectified by correcting the error into which Ptolemy and others were led by taking the length of the stades a great deal more than it should have been, namely, 600 stades to a degree of the Equator, instead of 500 stades, as has been done. Taking it at 500 stades (see Vivien St. Martin's *Africa:* Paris, 1843), and next the proportion to fix the breadth of the degree in the parallel of Alexandria (31° 12′), and we shall have the distance in longitude very nearly, indeed, correct, according to our mode of reckoning, that is, Alexandria 29° 53′; and the eastern source of the White Nile, according to Ptolemy, 4° 30′ more east, will be in 34° 23′, within a few miles of where Speke seeks to place it. Why, then, his coarse and unnecessary abuse of Ptolemy?

We return for a moment to Speke's Wahuma. That Adam was the head of the tribe no one will dispute. That they are descended from Europeans we leave our author to prove, and not to assert, reminding him that Japhet, the great progenitor of Europeans, was white, and that his Wahuma are black. He asserts that they are all descended from the great Jewish king David, while Zerah, the Ethiopian, was the next head of their tribe or race. Now, David's connection with them, if it existed, or ever could exist, could only be through Solomon and the Queen of Sheba, who came from African Ethiopia. From the death of David, 1014 A.C., to the accession of Solomon to the throne, in the same year, to the attack on Judah, by Zerah, in the reign of King Asa, 941 A.C., was a period of seventy-four years. The Queen of Sheba visited Solomon in the twenty-third year of his reign, consequently there remained only fifty-one years to produce from this connection a race, or in gaining the command of a people, mustering for a very distant war-field 1,000,000 fighting men. That Solomon's "Royal Bounty" to this celebrated Queen produced an heir to her throne is stated, and generally believed, in Eastern Tropical Africa, and may be readily admitted. But if this splendid, intelligent, and majestic Queen, Moqueda by name, had started up with Solomon in 1862, and seen the sable Queen Dowager Nyanamore "showing her broad stern" to the company while drinking pombe in company with her ministers and Captain Speke, pig fashion, both would, we are convinced, have indignantly disavowed the relationship, scattered the blockheads, and promptly dispelled the delusion.

Before quitting these pages, so filled with indecency, we may make one more quotation. The Queen Dowager had informed him "that she loved him much — loved him exceedingly!" Subsequently, at a meeting with her private Court Circle (p. 361), the conversation turned upon the capabilities of the women in the Royal Harem, when the attendants, laughing, asked Speke if he got a black wife, what the colour of the progeny by her would be. " The company became jovial, when the Queen improved it by making a significant gesture, with roars of laughter asking me (Speke) if I would like to be her son-in-law, for she had some beautiful daughters, either of the Wahuma or the Waganda breed! " Speke never should have allowed such narratives to have issued from his mouth, or stained his pages with such rubbish as this.

Further, a few words are necessary connected with the geography of Uganda. Speke does not give us the height of the hill on which the capital stood, but it is clear that the height is not great. We may, however, approximate it. It is 3,400 feet above the level of the sea; Namaouji, distant about 15 miles N.E. by E., is 3,103 feet. Murchison Creek, three or four miles west of the capital, is on a level with the lake, or nearly so, or say 290 feet below the summit of the hill. This will give the level of the creek at its junction with the lake to be 3,100 feet above the level of the sea, or 640 feet below the level of the lake at the Napoleon Inlet on the lake, and the same number of feet below the height of its southern shore! Between Murchison Creek and Napoleon Inlet, Speke was told that there were several great cataracts. How can there be any cataracts in the same lake, and how can the opposite shores of a lake be lower than the other shore of it, and how was one portion of the shore of the same lake higher than another portion of the same coast thereof? Can Captain Speke explain and clear up this confusion? *

Again, as regards the Mountains of the Moon, we have never met with any account, ancient or

---

* Captain Speke has six or seven outlets to his Lake Nyanza, all issuing from the north side and all running north, thus :—

1. The Mwerango River.

2. The River Myo Myanza joins the Mwerango.

3. Murchison Creek, which must be either the Myo Myanza or the Kitawana River, beside and near it several other streams.

4. The Luajerri River runs to the Nile.

5. The Nile from the Napoleon Channel.

6. Asua River, a river running from the north-east corner of Lake Nyanza, flowing N.W. to the Nile.

modern, pointing out in any manner why mountains in the quarter mentioned were or should be so designated. We believe the name proceeds from the following reason :—The moon is held in great reverence all over Tropical Africa. At the full moon it may truly be said that the whole population of Africa, old and young, are every night, for successive nights, engaged throughout it, singing, dancing, and feasting. Also everywhere when they speak of or point to a high mountain, they say " Moon Mountain ;" and when speaking of an exceeedingly high mountain they say " Moon, Moon Mountain." Hence, probably, the name of Mountain Range of the Moon for any very high hills or mountains throughout Tropical Africa.

Further about the moon. At page 243, and under dates January 5th and 6th, 1862, Speke informs us that :—" At night there was a partial eclipse of the moon. All the Wanguana marched up and down from Rumanika's to Nanaji's huts, singing and beating our tin cooking pots to frighten away the Spirit of the Sun from consuming entirely the chief object of their reverence, the moon." On consulting our astronomical authorities, we find that on the 17th December, 1861, there was a partial eclipse of the moon, and on the 31st December, 1861 (the same year), there was a total eclipse of the sun. Consequently there was not, and could not be, any eclipse of the moon, partial or otherwise, at the time stated by Captain Speke. The people of the real moon had a very hearty laugh at the story told, when the account reached them in due course. They were completely puzzled to account for the want of judgment shown by the author of the tale, trying, however, to account for it on the supposition that Captain Speke had a moon of his own, which he moved about like his "Mountains of the Moon," or else that he had abstracted and carried off Rumanika's moon in his pocket.

We may also here observe, in reference to the stated extent of the surface of Lake Nyanza, that the extent is given according to the reduced scale, taking it according to what Speke says he saw and heard in his first journey, and what he saw and heard in his second journey. As he has given it in his new work it is three times the extent that we have stated; this, consequently, if correct, makes his inconsistencies and errors more serious and reprehensible.

Before coming to a conclusion, we must notice a work, published at Edinburgh in 1810, by De Foe. Extracts from it have been sent to us by the Secretary of the Asiatic Society of Bombay. These give a concise account, so far, of a journey undertaken in 1720 from the East Coast of Africa, commencing in about 12° S. lat., with the intention of proceeding across the continent to the Congo in Angola. The journey is attributed to Captain Singleton and his ship's crew. They passed to the northward of Lake Nyassa, and thence proceeding they came to " a goodly river " running north, and from thence northwards and westwards till they came upon what must have been Lake Tanganyika, near its south end, as they struck it in 6·22° S. lat. After 23 days alongside of it northwards they rounded it, and then were told that they could not proceed westward to gain the Congo because another great lake lay in their way. They marched north along its western shore till they came to its end a little beyond the Equator, where they found a considerable river running north, which they set down as the

Nile, but not wishing to go by that route they turned to the westward, and finally, after many delays, taking from necessity different routes, they reached the Gold Coast. In the country to the north of the lake last mentioned they came upon a nation of negroes, who went, old and young, quite naked. They also met, in an uninhabited part, with a hideous serpent of fearful aspect and fangs, which threatened to attack them, and whose hissing was heard to a great distance. His men insisted that it was the Devil, but this he says could not, for a droll reason, be the case, because the Devil was not likely to be found in a country where there were no inhabitants. We have not ourselves seen this book, but the author of it seems to have written it with some knowledge of this portion of Africa. Here is, therefore, another claimant for the honour of the discovery of the sources of the White Nile.

Just as this part of our review was going to the press, we received the account that Petherick's accounts, journals, observations, and maps had reached this country, and at the same time the rash act, but to us anticipated act, of his deposition as British Consul. The following communication will tell us the sad consequences and the great injustice of the act. Petherick's letters in our hands also fully bear out all that this honest Belgian Consul states. We hasten to give the most material parts of his very able letter, thus :—

[TRANSLATION.]

"*Khartoum, Jan.* 28, 1864.

' A few days ago we received intelligence that the British Government had resolved to abolish the Consulate which it had established in the Soudan in 1849. That decision has troubled the honest portion of the colony, because, under the painful circumstances in which it is placed, it found in the experience and character of the British Consul a favourite rallying-point.

' A higher motive renders it desirable to maintain at Khartoum the British Consulate. The slave-traffic on the White Nile (for a long time held in restraint sufficiently feeble) has had for some years — thanks to the encouragement of certain high functionaries, who find their profit in it—an extension truly frightful ; and it is exercised with such horrors that I hesitate to describe them. Every year more than 100 vessels leave Khartoum for the purpose of hunting down the negroes; and slaves who formerly were brought in by stealth are now dragged publicly along the highways of the country, and even through the streets of Khartoum, with the yoke on their necks. The British Consul, Mr. J. Petherick, initiated measures which would have soon placed a limit to the traffic; unfortunately, owing to the aversion of four-fifths of the Khartoumians, who live by it, and of the high functionaries, their accomplices, he saw his reputation tarnished by false accusations; his fellow-citizens and friends misled on his account, and he found no sufficient support even before his superiors, who were doubtless thus prejudiced against him.

'The non-success of Mr. Petherick in his proceedings against certain persons accused of this traffic has given licence to these slave dealers. Assured henceforth of impunity and of the inefficiency of the law, they have thrown off the mask. It is an everlasting scandal to civilized Europe thus to authorise by her silence the infamous piracy which has stained the White Nile with blood; and for anti-slavery England, who instead of declaring herself impotent by abolishing her Consulate at Khartoum, should have surrounded it with all the *prestige* possible, authorised severe measures, and extended her hand to enforce their execution.

'Although personal considerations may be for us of secondary importance, and we are not the apologists of Mr. Petherick, we ought to add that the Consul—(a man of intelligence, and possessing a knowledge of the Soudan from a long experience)— has performed the duties of his office with an integrity and firmness which may well serve as an example to his colleagues. In the blow which has deprived Mr. Petherick of office, that which is the most distressing is the fact that his deposition followed quickly upon energetic measures taken by him against this traffic, and against that oppression which the local authorities endeavoured to bring to bear upon Europeans :—I repeat, this deposition of Mr. Petherick passes current through the country as a disavowal of those measures, and is regarded as a censure publicly inflicted upon Mr. Petherick by his superiors in consequence of the attitude he assumed.

'I am ignorant whether the British Government can now reconsider the decision it has taken ; but I do know that the re-establishment of a British Consulate at Khartoum would be a measure which all those who have at heart the triumph of the principles of civilization in this barbarous country would receive with joy.

(Signed) ' DE VRUYSSENAIRE.'

We shall not quote Petherick's own statements relating to these painful subjects, but show from another source the base accusations that were brought against him. We quote from a letter to him from Mr. Baker now before us, dated Feb. 9, 1863 :—

' I have much to say to you that I cannot write. There are serious intrigues against you in Khartoum. An accusation was sent to the Consul-General against you, signed by nearly all the Europeans of Khartoum, including the official declaration of two Consulates (who are they?), charging you with some former participation in slavery. Of course the seals of numerous natives ornamented the document.'

Well, let us now have the names of those knaves, more especially of the Consuls. We can guess them.

Did the Consul-General transmit that profligate accusation to Europe without placing it in Petherick's hands, and allowing him to answer it, and also without sending Petherick's slave-trade correspondence with him along with it? If he did all this, then it is the Consul-General and not the Consul that should have been dismissed. Again, did our Foreign Office, acting only upon the authority of the above infamous charge, dismiss a public servant without showing that servant the accusation brought against him, and without enabling him to vindicate himself? It would really appear that this is the course that has been adopted. Surely there are men in the Legislature who will call for the production of the papers and all the correspondence upon this important subject, in order that the British public may know the truth. In Khartoum there are only from 20 to 30 Europeans. Mr. Baker calls it a "horrid den!" and Dr. Murie says "they are chiefly low, rascally Frenchmen and Italians!" Is a British subject to be ruined and oppressed to please men like these?

This is a most unfortunate, a sad termination to the late great African exploration combination plan. But it is only such a termination as might have been anticipated from a scheme ill-contrived and most injudiciously carried on. That Captain Speke's unfounded charges against Consul Petherick influenced the Government and those to whom the Government looked up to for correct information and sound counsel, in short, in the quarter to which the Foreign Office looked to, scarcely any doubt can remain. How much, then, has Captain Speke to answer for, and how greatly is he to blame for the course he has pursued, and how bitterly must he feel, if he is capable of reflection, at the thoughts of the consequences which his flippant conduct and proceedings have produced. Here is the individual whom Speke urged to join and aid him in his journey,—the man whom the Foreign Office patronised, assisted, and permitted to lend his aid,—the energetic and experienced individual whom the Royal Geographical Society, through their proper authorities, encouraged, assisted, prompted, and selected as the most proper individual they could find to convey assistance and advice to Speke,—here, we say, is that

individual thrown overboard without pity, his private
fortune wasted, the health of himself and his heroic
and attached wife, altogether and perhaps irre-
trievably ruined, and his character as a merchant
and a public servant blasted in the eyes of his
countrymen and of the civilized world, by being
charged with a dereliction of duty, and with the
crime of slave dealing, at the moment he was doing
everything in his power to put it down.   Here are
all these ills heaped upon a poor man's head by
those who should have defended him; while Captain
Speke, whom he went to aid, and who never in all
his journey said one word against either slavery or
the slave trade, both of which he not only saw going
on before his eyes daily in all their horrors, but in
which it may almost be said he participated when
he accepted presents of female slaves as servants
"to carry his water," and after retaining them at
his pleasure, next handed them over thoughtlessly
to his Zanzibar assistants and followers as their
servants, to carry to Zanzibar, where they must
remain their slaves.   O Shame, where is thy blush !
O F * * * O * * * where is your judgment—where is
your justice !   You have injured innocence, and tar-

nished the great name of our country in the eyes of the world by the rash step you have taken; and no compensation that can now be given to Mr. Petherick can compensate him for the hardships, miseries, and losses that he has met with and sustained.

The fate which has overtaken Mr. Petherick will, we doubt not, prove a lesson to others who may be invited to join in similar undertakings, not to leave anything to chance, or to take everything for granted, with whomsoever they have to deal. Captain Speke will have full time to reflect upon his proceedings in this case. He left England on a great and noble enterprise. He was patronised and supported in it by the Government of India, by the British Government, and by the Royal Geographical Society, the greatest and most intelligent body of the kind in the world, and with the good wishes and with the sanguine hopes of the public. In return, what has he really gained and brought back? The sacrifice and ruin of zealous associates—a mass of intelligence, if such it can be called, so muddled and confused in everything that we really believe he himself cannot find his way in it. Nor is this all; he came back with tales of great empires and polished states in Africa, in order to enhance the glory of his reports, and to rouse the Government and the nation, upon the accuracy of his reports, to lay hold of those parts in order to extend our power and our commerce. The public for a time was beside itself with those fascinating dreams. The whole has turned out mere moonshine. Those great empires have dwindled to atoms; barbarous, rude, savage, and ignorant beyond all precedent and example. Instead of commerce, fleets, and armies at their command, these wretched chiefs cannot muster a few hundreds of men, or glean ten recruits at a time to increase their armies.

Finally, we deeply regret the miserable termination which this great African exploration expedition has had. We regret it on the part of the public, and we sincerely lament the result on account of Captain Speke himself. It might, it ought to have been different. But the only person to blame for the poor results is Captain Speke himself. We truly lament the time that has been lost, and the money that has been spent, without any definite settlement of any material point, and with only the absurd result of finding the source of the great river Nile placed in a narrow ravine, where not a drop of water is to be found, except that which drops from the clouds during the periodical rains— nay, chiefly the fresh water which rushes into this ravine from the flooding of the lake to the north-ward, and which flood flows in an opposite direction to the current of the true Nile stream!

THE END.